—THE—
FLOWER
WORKSHOP

THE FLOWER WORKSHOP

Ideas and instructions for
handmade flowers and plants

Vera Jeffery

with photographs by Malcolm Lewis

Hearst Books
New York

Copyright © 1980 Vera Jeffery
and Malcolm Lewis/London Editions

Designed and produced by
London Editions Limited,
9 Long Acre, London WC2E 9LH

Line drawings by Terri Lawlor
and Andrew Farmer

First published in USA 1980 by
Hearst Books
224 W.57 St., New York, NY 10019

Library of Congress Catalog Card
Number 79–89824

ISBN 0–87851–203–9

Printed in Italy

4

Contents

Introduction

Author's note

Having lived my whole life in the countryside I have always loved fresh flowers and realize that nothing can equal their beauty, but I also get a tremendous thrill from making a flower in paper or fabric as close as possible to the real flower which was its inspiration.

To me the flowers I make are never artificial. They are very real, because I have created them, and they are just as much an art form as is a painting or a piece of sculpture from life. So, for me personally, they are not simply a substitute for real flowers, although many of the pictures in the book illustrate ideas which could well use either. For this reason I do feel that paper, fabric and wax flowers must fit the occasion for which they are made and the occasion must be right for them.

It is always exciting to experiment with the different techniques for making flowers. I quickly discovered that the colors and texture of crêpe paper could be made so much more interesting by dampening the paper and squeezing it together with other shades so that the final appearance was as though it has been delicately hand painted. This is described in detail as one of the basic techniques to learn before you start to make your first flower.

When you are leafing through the pages and wondering which flower to try first I do advise you, particularly if you are a beginner, that it is essential to make, or at least to read carefully, the basic steps for a paper rose and a fabric poppy in this introductory section. For here we have covered the basic techniques you need to go on to make any of the flowers in the book. Then, I am sure, you too will find it easy.

I have made thousands of flowers and I never tire of making them. There always seems something new to discover and each time there is the fascination of wondering how lifelike it will be. I do hope you will enjoy this book and the flowers you will feel inspired to make and that, having mastered the basic steps, you will feel encouraged to experiment, as I did, and learn more.

Vera Jeffery.

Tools and equipment

Adhesive Any type, suitable for fabric and paper, which dries clearly and quickly.

Bleach Use a household bleach. It can be applied with a thin brush or, if fine lines like veins are required, a pen or knitting needle can be dipped in the bleach and used. It tends to spread on fabric so use carefully.

Brushes Use a small household paint brush for applying size or starch to fabric and a thin artist's paint brush for tinting the edges of petals.

Cardboard Use to make templates. It should be the thickness of a postcard.

Cotton wool (cotton) Use for buds or the center of flowers, such as the rose and poppy.

Crayons For flower markings, a crayon or oil-based pastel is best for the harder outlines, and a soft pastel for shading.

Drawing (or T) pins Use to pin material to board for sizing or starching. They should be rustproof.

Dyes For coloring fabrics.

Fabrics Velvet and velveteen, cotton, organdie, silk, taffeta, organza and satin, but no wholly synthetic fabrics, can be used in making flowers.

Felt-tip pens A set of these pens is useful to have for putting pollen spots or markings on such flowers as lilies and rhododendrons.

Floral tape Use for winding around stems. It is used in making fabric flowers and small paper ones. Comes in several colors.

Foam rubber A small piece 5cm (2in.) thick is used as a base when cupping fabric petals with a heated spoon.

Inks (colored) These are useful for tinting materials or edges of paper petals or for coloring twine stamens.

Iron Use for pressing fabrics.

Knitting needle Use for curling petal edges. It should be metal so that it can be heated.

Nail-brush Use in preparing crêpe paper to dampen the cut pieces.

Paint Poster paint or watercolor can be used for coloring twine stamens or for painting centers on fabric flowers, such as polyanthus. Poster paint can be thinned.

Paper Always use a good quality crêpe paper for the best results. Double-sided crêpe paper is excellent for some flowers, such as magnolia and the water lily. Multi-layered paper napkins are used to make carnations. Metallic papers can be used for Christmas or fun flowers.

Pastels Artist's pastels are best for coloring petals where a soft shaded effect is desired.

Pencils Use to draw around templates.

Pinking shears Use sometimes to trim edges of flower petals, like the carnation, or leaves, like the hydrangea.

Pipe cleaners These make excellent stamens for the arum and tiger lily and also form the center of a fabric daisy.

Pliers A small pair of (needle-nosed) pliers is essential for making the tiny hook at the end of the stem which holds the stamen in some flowers, such as the African violet. Pliers can also be used for cutting and bending wire.

Potting materials A flower pot in a size to suit the plant. To support the flowers or plant place florist's foam in the flower pot.

Rubber gloves Wear these when dyeing materials or when squeezing together dampened pieces of crêpe paper.

Ruler (or tape measure) For measuring paper and fabric.

Saucepan Use for melting wax. It should be deep enough to allow the entire flower head to be covered when dipped in the wax.

Saucer Use for holding bleach and for mixing poster paints.

Scissors For cutting out the parts of the flower from paper or fabric. Use a small pair of scissors for the smaller flowers and florets, such as the violet and hydrangea. Also use the scissor-blade to curl the edges of petals—again use small scissors for the small petals. The point of the scissor-blade can also be used to score veins in the leaves.

Sisal twine This is a twine made up of many fine strands and is excellent for fringing out for stamens. The ends can be dipped in ink or paint to color them. Twine can be bought at hardware stores and garden and agricultural suppliers.

Size A stiffening agent to brush onto fabric to strengthen it and to prevent the edges from fraying, before making the flower. A small pack of size (wallpaper paste) will last a long time as it is only used in very small quantities.

Sizing board This is the board onto which the fabric is pinned before sizing. Any strong, clean board will do; a pastry board or very strong cardboard can be used.

Spoons Use for cupping petals which have first been sprayed with starch. Heat the spoon by placing in very hot water. The size of the spoon depends on the size of the petal, but a deep spoon is best; for small petals use a salt or mustard spoon. A melon scoop can be used for larger petals.

Stamens There are various types of stamens; either buy the small-headed ones from a hobby shop or make your own from crêpe paper, covered wire, pipe cleaners or sisal twine.

Starch Household starch should be mixed and then brushed onto fabric to stiffen it and prevent the edges from fraying, before making the flower. Starch can be bought in an aerosol can and we use this for spraying on petals before cupping them.

Templates These are the pattern shapes made from thin cardboard. Place them on the fabric or paper and cut around.

Tracing paper Use to make templates, by tracing the pattern from the book and transferring it to thin cardboard. Greaseproof (waxed) paper can be used.

Varnish Spray on paper leaves to darken them and make them shine. Use an artist's varnish for oil paintings which comes in an aerosol can. Hair spray can be used as a substitute.

Wax Use for waxing paper and some fabric flowers. Buy plain, colorless candle wax or paraffin wax from a hobby shop.

Wire Various thicknesses of wire are needed for flower making. In general, a fine wire is needed to bind the base of the petals and support the leaves, and a stronger wire is used for the stems. Wire netting (chicken wire) can be used in garlands or in the bottom of a vase to support large floral arrangements.

Wire cutters Use for cutting wire. Can be substituted by pliers.

Preparing your materials

Paper

Crêpe paper, which comes in a variety of beautiful colors as well as white, can, if you wish, be made even more exciting in color and texture by a very simple process which also makes the flowers look very natural.

The purpose of the process is simply to allow the strong colors of one shade of paper to run into another shade by wetting them and squeezing them together. A single color can also be dampened and squeezed to give it a crinkly effect.

The joy of this is that you can experiment and invent your own color combinations which you may choose either for their likeness to the natural flower or because of their more bizarre but colorful effect. Where this tinting is particularly effective, or necessary to achieve the correct resemblance to the real flower, we have stated that prepared paper should be used at the beginning of the instructions for that flower.

A good supply of paper can be tinted and prepared in advance if you know that you are intending to make several flowers at a time. For example, the three strips of paper shown being tinted in the photographs will be sufficient to make six roses in varying shades of red through to pink.

To prepare the paper you will need:
Crêpe paper in a choice of three colors that you think will blend well together (shown here: pink, white, red)
A saucer of water
Small nail-brush
Rubber gloves

Take one of the three colors of crêpe paper (shown here: pink) and holding the paper, still folded as in the packet, cut through the several thicknesses to cut off a 10cm (4in.) piece that will eventually unfold into a long strip about 240cm (8ft) long. One strip makes two roses.

Repeat this for the other two colors (red and white).
Using a draining board or waterproof surface and wearing rubber gloves, hold the pink, white and red pieces together with the edges level and dip the cut ends into the water in the saucer up to 1cm ($\frac{1}{2}$in.) in depth.

Laying each color flat, dampen the cut pieces further using a small nail-brush as shown.

Place the three colors together again and, holding them in both hands, gently squeeze the water out.

This step is to make the different colors of crêpe paper run together. This slightly changes the tint of the paper and gives a variegated effect. To dry these pieces lay them down flat in a warm atmosphere, for example in a very slow oven on a baking sheet.
When dry the paper will have interesting markings and a crinkly texture which looks very natural.

To see the effect in a finished flower, see pages 13 and 22.

Fabric

When making flowers out of fabric, use any scraps you may have left over from dressmaking. If you need to buy fabric, a guide to the length of material you require is as follows: approximately ½ metre (½yd) for the larger plants, such as a spider plant, ⅛–¼ metre (⅛–¼yd) for the small flowers, such as violets and polyanthus.

This is only a rough guide as the amount of fabric also depends on how big a plant or flower you wish to make and how many. If you wish to know more precisely how much fabric to buy, you can work it out by laying the templates on newspaper, folded to the width of the fabric, and multiplying the amount of fabric required for one flower by the number of flowers you wish to make.

For green plants which have veins marked in bleach, such as ivy, use a home-dyed fabric, since the bleach does not always have the desired effect on factory-dyed fabric. Use old white sheets and pillow-cases, if you have them, and dye them green.

To color fabric

The main method of coloring fabrics is to dye them. The dyes that are available are in liquid or in powder form, to be mixed with hot or cold water. Make sure that you choose a dye which is suitable for the type of fabric you will be using. The amount you need is shown in the instructions and depends on the amount of fabric you want to dye.

For dyeing you will need a rustproof vessel—and one that can be heated if you happen to be using a hot water dye. It must be deep, too, to allow the fabric to be completely immersed.

Dyes may be mixed to produce your own colors or used on their own, but whatever colors you choose, make sure you follow the instructions carefully. This means testing a piece of the fabric first to see the results. If this is done, nothing should go wrong.

There are many different effects which can be achieved with dyeing. Perhaps the most useful for flowercraft is the tie-dye method, where the piece of fabric is rolled up and several knots tied in it, before dipping it in the dye; this produces a variegated color. For a pale and natural-looking tint, dip the fabric in dye, then wring it and allow to dry.

A simple rule to remember is that the longer the fabric remains in the dye, the deeper the color will be.

Fabrics are usually dyed first and stiffened afterwards, but white silk can be colored after sizing, with broad felt-tip pens. In this way you can vary the depth of the color on the silk. You can put colored markings on all fabric flowers, once they are made up, with paint or ink or using felt-tip pens.

To stiffen fabric

It is important that the fabric is stiffened before starting to make the flowers. This gives body to the finished flower as well as preventing the edges of petals and leaves from fraying. Fabric can be stiffened with size or starch.

Buy a small pack of decorator's size or household starch and mix according to instructions. For a 45cm (½yd) length of fabric use approximately ½ pint of size and water. The strength of the mixture depends on the fabric. The sheer fabrics such as silk, taffeta and fine cotton only require a weak mix. The heavier fabrics like satin and velvet need a stronger solution; one which will not soak through the fabric and ruin the surface. A little glue can be added to the starch, if desired.

Attach the fabric right side down to a board with four drawing pins, one at each corner. The sizing board can be of wood or thick cardboard. Use a household paint brush to spread the size or starch evenly over the fabric, smoothing out any unevenness caused by air bubbles, and removing any excess size with a damp sponge or cloth. Leave to dry in a warm place. (See pictures below.)

If you are using cardboard as a sizing board be careful that the fabric does not stick to it when dry. Removing the bottom two drawing pins, lean the board at a slight angle against a wall so that the fabric hangs straight down, but away from the board while drying.

The flower center

The stamens and pistils which form the flower centers, however tiny and seemingly insignificant compared with the showy petals, are nevertheless the part of the finished flower which gives it its character and also offers the flower maker the greatest opportunity to be inventive. Numerous materials are suitable for flower centers—and it is as well to prepare a batch of stamens in advance if making a large number of the same flower. Those suggested in the instructions for each flower are the ones we have found most suitable, but you should go on experimenting for different effects. Some of the alternatives are listed below :
The **stamens** bought **from a hobby shop** are small-headed and can be used singly as the center of a small flower or in a bunch for a large flower like a rose.

Wire stamens can be made from thread-covered wire, which comes in various colors, and a pistil from a piece of twisted wire, with a loop at one end, covered in a crêpe paper, as in the orchid (see right).

Paper stamens are either made from a fringed strip of crêpe paper, the ends twisted into strands between your finger and thumb, or a narrow strip of paper sprayed with starch tightly rolled up and allowed to dry. The latter could be used in a narcissus or daffodil.

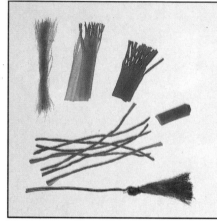

Another type of flower center, as in a daisy, can be made by cutting a long strip of crêpe paper, folding it in half lengthways and rolling it into a short thick cylinder. The top of the cylinder forms the flat, coiled center. **Sisal twine stamens** are made by cutting a small piece of twine and separating one end out into strands, which can be dipped in ink or paint to color them, if desired, as in the fabric poppy.

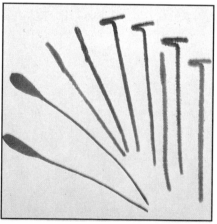

A pipe cleaner stamen or pistil is made by bending over the end and twisting it into the rest of the pipe cleaner, or bending it to the characteristic shape for a particular flower, as in the madonna lily.
A small tight ball of **cotton wool** (cotton), dipped in glue and placed at the end of a 3.5cm (1½in.) length

of No. 4 or 5 wire, when left to dry and harden, can then be colored by dipping into yellow poster paint or ink. These are a suitable alternative to stamens from a hobby shop, though it is difficult to make them quite as small and neat as the bought ones.
Dried seed heads such as those of the poppy or teazel, or a small bunch of florets from an achillea flower head, make very effective flower centers, and these can either be left in their natural state, or be painted or sprayed with glitter for Christmas.
Buttons and large **beads** make ideal centers for fun flowers. The button can be dabbed with glue, dipped in glitter, allowed to dry and then threaded through the center of a large flat flower, such as a poinsettia sprayed with gold. A large wooden

bead can be threaded on wire, looped to prevent the bead falling off. A single one or a few in a bunch are suitable for the center of an open flower with cupped petals, such as the metallic rose.

Patterns

Wire

Some flowers, such as the paper rose or peony, are simply made from winding up a single strip of crêpe paper; others require a pattern for their petals. The patterns are given as outlines for the correct shape of the leaf, petal, stamens or calyx. When all four have to be cut out, all the patterns are given.

It is easy to make a template by tracing the pattern from the book onto cardboard (see page 14). When using the template to cut out the flower shapes, make sure that the grain of the paper is running the way it is indicated on the pattern. All patterns for flowers which can be made up in crêpe paper show the direction of the grain, which is indicated by three parallel lines.

A short cut to making several identical petals at the same time is to fold the fabric into several thicknesses and cut the shape through all these. This is a very useful technique for making a flower which consists of many small florets, such as a hydrangea, or of several pairs of leaves, such as a palm frond.

All the patterns in the book, except one exceptionally long leaf for the gladioli, are given in the actual size for the made-up flower. However you should feel free to make the flower bigger or smaller, as you prefer. And this applies to the shape of the flower, too. As you begin to feel more confident, you will probably not need to trace the patterns from the book, but draw the shape freehand straight onto the card.

You can even make your own patterns from real flowers. Take the petals off a rose or any other flower and make up your own templates by following their shapes. Once you get involved in flowercraft you will find innumerable ways of making petals, leaves, centers and the rest. Our book is only the start.

Perhaps the most essential item for flowercraft, apart from the paper or fabric, is the wire which you will need to give the flower its support and structure. You are advised to buy this in advance as it is one of the few items needed which you may not have among your household things, though a wire coat hanger might suffice for the heavier wire and you may well have some fine electrical wire for the most delicate flowers.

Wires are usually identified by gauge, which is the measurement of their diameter or thickness, and this determines their different functions for flower making. For example, the heavier or thicker wires in straight lengths are used for strong stems, the finer wires for binding the base of the petals without causing bulk, or for the stems of small delicate flowers or leaves.

The types of wire needed in this book are those that you will be able to buy either from a hobby shop, a hardware store, a florist or, perhaps, an electrical store. This wire is uncovered wire which you will cover, during the course of making the flower, either with green crêpe paper for a paper flower (see page 13), or with floral tape for a fabric flower (see page 16) and small paper ones. It is also possible to buy a fine thread-covered wire from a hobby shop. This is most suitable for fabric flowers and can be substituted for wire and floral tape.

The table with wires numbered from 1 to 5 has been devised specially for this book in order that you will not be confused by the different ways wire is described in the shops. The numbers are only for identification for the correct wire in relation to the instructions given in this book; they will mean nothing to a shopkeeper. The numbers 1 to 5 denote the five grades of wire from the thickest to the finest and you should use this chart simply as a guide for yourself when buying or preparing wire. Don't be too worried about getting the exact thickness, however, and you don't have to follow our recommendations rigidly; you may wish to use a finer wire than we have suggested for binding the calyx in some cases, for instance. You will soon find which wire you can obtain most easily and work with best.

Nos. 1 and 2 are used for the main stem of a flower or plant. For a large plant the heavier No. 1 wire is best, but in most cases Nos. 1 and 2 are interchangeable.
No. 3 is important for binding stamens, flower bases, and for forming the stems of leaves and some petals, and the main stems of smaller flowers. It is also used to bind the main stem of a flower to a strong stick or piece of cane.
Nos. 4 and 5 are used for binding the bases of the smaller flowers, such as the violet, and can sometimes be substituted for No. 3 wire.

The American wire gauge equivalents are as follows :
No. 1–14, No. 2–16, No. 3–18, No. 4–20, No. 5–28.

1	●━━━━━━━━━━━━━━━━━━━━━	1
2	●────────────────	2
3	·────────────────	3
4	·────────────────	4
5	. ────────────────	5

Basic steps for flower making

The two examples of the paper rose and the fabric poppy on the following pages represent the two basic methods of flower making used in this book, and they will cover in more detail here the techniques you will encounter in specific flowers described later. It is essential that you try these two examples first in order to learn the basic steps. Read through all the instructions before starting. Then you are well on your way to an enjoyable and rewarding time and should feel encouraged to go on and develop your own ideas in trying out different flowers from those in this book.

Not *all* paper flowers are wound up from a single strip of paper. Some use a pattern and can be made in exactly the same way as the fabric flower example given. Nearly all the flowers can be made in either paper or fabric, and many can be waxed, but you will be given a guide about this in the introduction to the instructions for each flower.

For a paper flower: a rose

The example of a rose is shown on the following pages because it illustrates the basic steps for making a paper flower which does not need a pattern or individual petal parts. The flower head is simply folded from one long, specially prepared strip of crêpe paper. The paper has been tinted as shown on page 8. By making the rose the beginner will be introduced to the basic techniques for cutting and curling the petal shapes, making the sepals and covering the stem of a paper flower. If you have never attempted flower making before, the rose is a marvellously rewarding and easy flower to try for the first time. (If you want to go on to make a fabric rose, turn to page 24.)

For a paper rose you will need:
Prepared crêpe paper for petals
Suggested colors: red, pink, yellow and white
Green crêpe paper
No. 1 and No. 3 wire
Scissors
Knitting needle or meat skewer
Wire cutters
Quick-drying clear glue

Step 1 To cut the petal shapes
Take one prepared and dried strip of paper 10cm (4in.) deep, still folded as in the packet, and cut out two scallop shapes from the crinkled edge. Start cutting halfway up one side and round off the corner. Repeat other side.

Make a shallow V-shaped cut in the center of this to form two equal petal shapes.

This gives a series of petal shapes when you unfold the strip of paper.

Step 2 To curl and cup the petals
With the strip of petals unfolded and taking each petal one at a time, curl the edge around the meat skewer or knitting needle once or twice. Take care to curl all the petals in the same direction, inwards, but alternate the slant of the curls as shown.

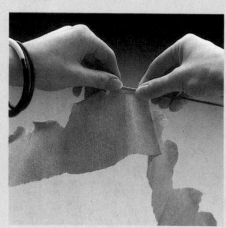

Continue doing this for 120cm (4ft), which is halfway along the paper strip, then cut off the remaining half and set aside, as only half a strip is needed for each rose.
Holding each petal with both hands so that the petal curls away from you, stretch across the center of the petal with your thumbs to make it cup away from you.

Choose at this point which end of the petal strip has the prettiest markings, which you would like to show on the inside of your flower. (It is often most effective to have the darkest colorings at the center of the flower.)
Continue cupping the petals all along the strip.

Step 3 To make the flower head
Starting with the end which will be in the center of the flower, begin to roll up the petal strip, firmly holding the base in the other hand.
To continue, you will need to pleat the paper at the base between the petal shapes to make the petals appear to grow outwards as the flower becomes fuller. Make sure that the center of the flower is level with the outside petals, otherwise it will pull out after winding.

Basic steps for flower making

Still holding the flower firmly, wind No. 3 wire very tightly three times around the base where the paper is gathered.

Cut the wire.
Twist the ends together.

Step 4 To make the stem
Cut a piece of No. 1 wire 30cm (12in.) long, or according to the desired height of your flower, and bend the end over with pliers to form a small hook 1cm (½in.) in length.
Pierce the center of the flower and push the wire down through the flower, leaving the hook embedded in the center to hold it in place.

Step 5 To make the sepals
Cut a piece of green crêpe paper 10cm (4in.) wide and 11cm (4½in.) long.
Mark off the 11cm (4½in.) side into six equal parts and fold the paper at the places you have marked to get six thicknesses.
Cut this thin strip into a shallow point at one end.
Unfold the strip to get a six-pointed sepal shape.

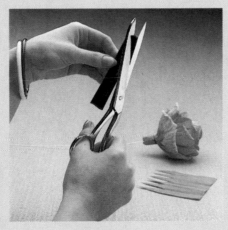

Apply a little glue to the base of the flower and attach one end of the sepal strip securely.
Wrap the sepals around the flower base to cover it completely and glue down the other edge.

Step 6 To cover the stem
Cut a piece from a roll of green crêpe paper 2.5cm (1in.) wide which will open out into a long green strip.
Put a little glue on the outside of the sepal base.
Attach one end of the green strip to the sepal base and wind it around the base several times very tightly, pressing the paper close to the wire.
Hold the paper strip in one hand and the flower stem in the other between your thumb and forefinger.
Rotate the flower as you wind the green stem paper tightly down the wire stem, stretching the paper slightly as you wind.

This is difficult at first but gets easier with practice and is worth perfecting as a technique.
Tear the paper off at the bottom of the stem.
Glue the end securely, making sure that all the wire is covered neatly.
Now you have a finished flower.

For a fabric flower: a poppy

The detailed step-by-step instructions given here for the fabric poppy will introduce the basic techniques for making a fabric flower and leaves. The most important difference between this and the previous example of the paper rose is that the flower is assembled from individual petal shapes which are cut out from a template. Once you have mastered the technique for doing this on this simple example, you will be able to make any of the flowers in this book using templates, and even perhaps go on to make up your own templates for flowers not included. The technique for cupping fabric petals, different from the technique for paper, is also demonstrated here. (If you want to try a paper poppy, turn to page 29.)

For a fabric poppy you will need:
Fine cotton fabric, silk, rayon or organza that has been stiffened with starch or size sufficiently to be almost papery when dry (see p. 9). This is for the petals.
Suggested colors: bright red, shades of pink, burgundy or yellow
Light green cotton fabric for leaves
No. 1 and No. 3 wire
Tracing paper
Thin cardboard for template
Pencil and black felt-tip pen
Cotton wool (cotton)
Sisal twine
Deep teaspoon or melon scoop
A cup of boiling water
Scissors
Quick-drying clear glue
Wire cutters
Green floral tape
Starch (in an aerosol can)
Foam rubber sponge

Step 1 To make the template
Trace pattern 1, which is at the bottom of this page, onto tracing paper.

Transfer this pattern onto thin cardboard, first by scribbling with pencil on the back of the pattern. Then turn the tracing paper over so that the pencilled side is against the cardboard and re-trace the pattern.

The shape will then be transferred to the cardboard. Cut out.
This is your petal template.

Step 2 To make the petals
Place template on prepared material, trace around it and cut out.
For this poppy you will need four petals, so it is time-saving to fold your prepared fabric into four thicknesses and cut out four petals at the same time. This also ensures that all the petal shapes are identical, which is not so important in the poppy as the petals are used singly, but when you come to make pairs of leaves and petals which are to be glued directly on top of each other, it is essential.

Mark the petals with a black felt-tip pen from the base to a third of the way up the petal.

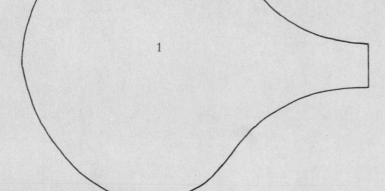

1

Step 3 To make the flower center and stamens

Cut two pieces of sisal twine 7.5cm (3in.) long and separate one end of each into strands 5cm (2in.) down. Color these ends with black ink 2.5cm (1in.) down the twine.

Cut a circle 5cm (2in.) in diameter from light green cotton fabric. Make a ball of cotton wool (cotton) about the size of a large pea and wrap the circle of fabric around it, bunching up the ends at the bottom.

Group the stamens around the green ball, holding the uncolored ends of the twine with the bunched-up green fabric, and bind with one twist of No. 3 wire to secure them.

Trim the tips of the black stamens to the same length and make sure they are evenly spaced around the green ball.

Step 4 To cup the petals

Spray the petals with starch to thoroughly dampen them.
Take one petal and place it on the dry foam rubber sponge.
Using a deep teaspoon or melon scoop, which has been heated by standing for a few minutes in boiling water and then dried, press down and round into the petal to cup it. Repeat for all petals.
Edges of spoons sometimes leave marks, so it is best to use the most completely rounded metal object you have in the kitchen.

Step 5 To assemble flower head and stem.

Put a touch of glue on each petal base.
Place first two petals opposite each other around the stamens and centre and press in firmly at base. Place the other two petals alternately opposite these.

Still holding petals firmly together at base, wind round with two or three twists of No. 3 wire to secure. Then proceed as overleaf.

Cut a length of No. 1 wire for stem 30cm (12in.) long and make a small hook at one end.

Pull the wire down into the flower to one side of the green center, making sure that the hook becomes firmly embedded in flower base without showing.

Wind floral tape around the base of the petals to form the calyx, cover the binding wire, and continue winding down the stem wire to cover it neatly.

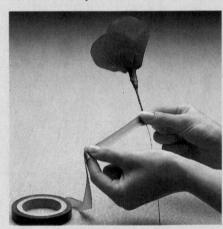

Step 6 To make leaf

Trace template from pattern 2 using tracing paper and thin cardboard as for petal template.

Cut the leaf shape in a double-thickness of green cotton fabric to make two identical shapes.

Cut a length of No. 3 wire 5cm (2in.) longer than the leaf and cover neatly with floral tape.

Dab glue all around one leaf shape and down the center.

Place covered wire along the line of glue in the center of the leaf. Take up the other leaf shape and fit it exactly over the glued leaf and wire and press in place. If the edges do overlap at any point, trim with scissors.

Mark veins on the front of the leaf with a scissor-blade or a knitting needle as shown.

Step 7 To assemble the flower and leaves

Twist wire of leaf to flower stem halfway down and bend leaf over gently away from flower. Cover join with floral tape, if desired.

2

Waxed flowers

Many real flowers have a wax-like sheen on their petals, such as those of the magnolia or tulip. You may decide to wax the flowers after you have made them either because you wish to capture this naturalistic sheen of the real flower or simply for the effect of waxing for its own sake. For an example of the latter, the tiny wild violet is exquisitely delicate and beautiful with a translucent glass-like quality when waxed—a small vase of them can almost look like a delicate glass ornament.

Paper flowers are more suitable for waxing than fabric, as the fabric in general is used for its own texture and effect and should not need waxing. However, small flowers from thin cotton fabric can be waxed successfully.

Waxed flowers tend to deteriorate quickly if worn or handled a lot as the wax cracks, so for buttonholes and trimmings for hats and dresses, waxed flowers are not suitable. Waxed flowers look particularly lovely in the floral arrangements under glass which the Victorians liked so much and in smaller arrangements in a vase on a table, or as shown in the subsequent pages.

Buy plain, colorless candle or paraffin wax which comes in a block from a hobby shop. Use a can, wide and deep enough to hold the flower head, and put in enough wax to cover the flower head completely when you are ready to wax it. (Do not put the flower in yet.) A little glycerine can be added to the wax to prevent cracks in the waxed flower— one teaspoon to $\frac{1}{2}$ pint of melted wax is sufficient. Put the can in a saucepan with a little water. Heat until the wax has melted. Then switch off the heat and remove the saucepan to a heatproof surface. Always be careful when using wax as it is highly inflammable.

Put on a pair of household rubber gloves and, holding the stem, dip the whole flower head, completely covering it, into the hot wax and keep it there for a few seconds.

Take out carefully, making sure that the wax has covered the flower thinly and evenly. Shake gently over a newspaper to get rid of any excess wax and to avoid large drops of it drying on the petals.

Attach the stem of the flower to a clothes line, with a clothes pin or by twisting the stem around it. Let it hang free to allow it to dry evenly. If a line is not easily available, put the flowers gently onto paper to dry.

Before the wax has dried completely and while the petals are still pliable you may need to re-arrange them carefully if they have been misshapen or bent at all during the waxing. Avoid using the fingers to do this—a metal object is best, if you want to retain the translucent quality of the wax.

If your waxed flowers do begin to look a little world-weary, you can always revive them again by re-waxing. This will make them look as good as new.

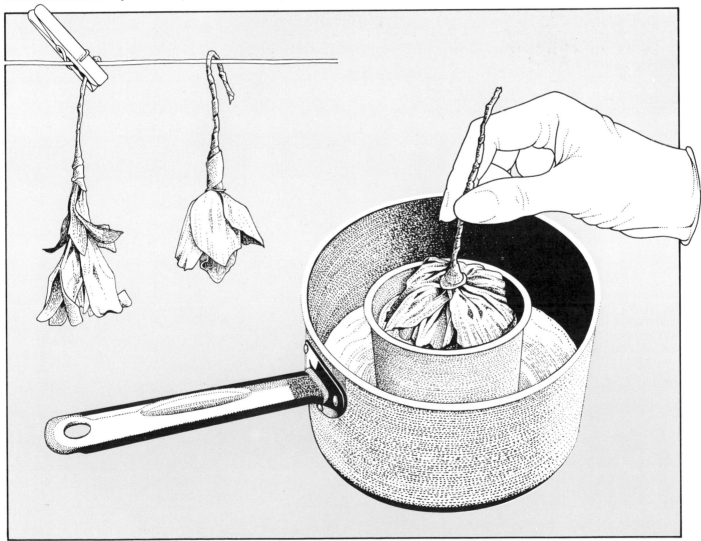

Above *A picture frame or mirror is lovely trimmed with flowers and these waxed flowers seem nostalgically appropriate for this corridor with its walls lined with old family portraits. The flowers are firmly attached to the back of the mirror with clear tape. The stems are then bent to bring the flower heads to the front of the picture in the way in which you want to arrange them.*

Right *These small flowers, which have been waxed to sit prettily in this china basket, were all made from paper before waxing. The finished effect is almost like a china and glass ornament. Rosebuds, orange and apple blossom as well as stephanotis have been used.*

A Glass Dome of Waxed Flowers

The Victorians made marvellous arrangements under glass using, among other things, dried flowers, grasses, artificial birds and butterflies. These have inspired modern displays today. The glass dome here is filled with miniature flowers which have been waxed to give them a translucence particularly pretty when light shines from behind the dome. Waxing flowers also helps them retain their newness.

If you wish to make this arrangement, you will find a glass dome in an antique or hobby shop. However you may wish to use the more modern glass plant cases that are now available.

Fix a spiked flower holder (usually used at the bottom of a vase) to the base of the dome with glue or clay. Onto this fix a block of florist's foam. Make it into a cone reaching halfway up the dome and leaving enough space around the sides at the base for small flowers and leaves.

Choose the flowers you wish to make, but make them in miniature. We have used roses, daisies, arum and tiger lilies, poppies and mixed them with dried grasses. Decide which flowers you would like at the top of the dome and make their stems the longest. The flowers at the bottom and sides will have short stems. Make several leaves of different sizes.

Wax the flowers and leaves. When they are ready you can make your arrangement. Use the leaves to fill in the spaces between the flowers and to cover the florist's foam. This is particularly important at the bottom of the dome where the foam is most likely to show.

You will then have created a beautiful display which will give you pleasure for a long time to come.

The flowering plant
What you need to know for flower making

When making paper or fabric flowers take a close look at the real ones for inspiration and information. The instructions in this book are detailed and give you all that you need to know to be able to make the flowers illustrated, but it is always helpful to have an understanding of the functions of the different parts. If you wish to develop the designs further, or make your own patterns for different flowers, you can more easily do so with an understanding of the relation of the different parts of a real plant.

The parts of the flower

This diagrammatic representation of a section through a flower shows in simple terms the main parts of the flower in relation to each other. The shapes and relative sizes of these will vary from one flower to another.

A few technical terms

Flute To give a wavy edge to a paper petal or leaf, by stretching the edge, thereby making it crinkle, as in the trumpet-shaped center of the narcissus and daffodil.
Fringe To make a row of narrowly spaced slits on the edge of the paper or fabric you are using. This is one of the main methods of making stamens for flowers, as in the poppy or apple blossom.
Pleat To make a fold by doubling part of a length of fabric or paper in on itself. When winding round a long petal strip to form a peony or rose, for example, make little pleats at the base of the flower to make it less bulky and to help the strip fold round more easily.
Score To make indentations with the point of an instrument, such as scissors or knitting needle, to mark veining on leaves, for instance.

1 Petal
The petals of a real flower are usually conspicuous and brightly colored in order to attract insects which carry the pollen. They are, of course, the loveliest part of the flower and you should make the petals of your flowers as beautiful and as showy as possible.

2 Calyx and sepals
The calyx, which is a collection of green sepals, protects the flower at bud stage. Once the flower has opened it may still be a decorative feature of the flower, at the point where the petals join the stem.

3 Stamens
The stamens are the male part of the flower and these produce pollen grains and are thus often powdery at their tips.

4 Pistil
The pistil, which is the female part of the flower, is usually identifiable as the most central part of the flower.
Sometimes it is difficult to distinguish the stamens and pistils from each other when they appear as a large flat flower center, as in the marguerite daisy.

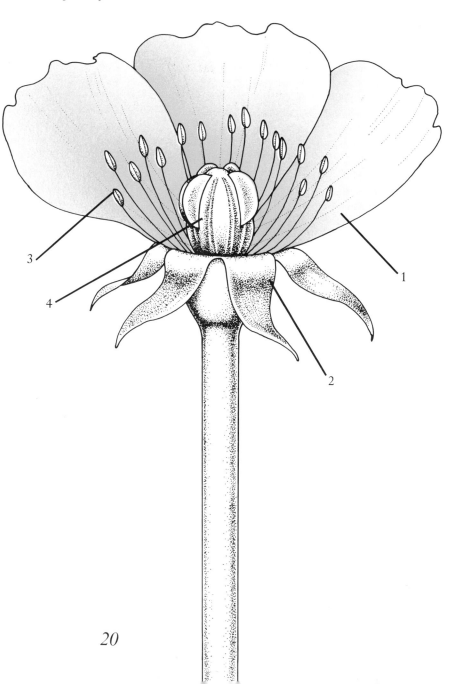

Leaves and leaf stems

The leaves and stems, their shapes and the positions into which they are bent for the finishing touches, contribute more to the final success of your flower or plant than you might at first expect. Thus it is important to take just as much care with the foliage as you do with the blooms themselves.

When making the leaves, you usually make the supporting wire a little longer than the leaf shape and cover it with green crêpe paper for a paper leaf, or floral tape for a fabric leaf. This supporting wire therefore also forms the leaf stem.

Leaf stems can be twisted onto the already covered main stem of the plant, or they can be twisted onto the uncovered main stem and bound over with a crêpe paper strip or floral tape. The narrower the strip of paper, the neater the end result will be.

Leaf stems can show or not, according to your preference or the type of flower you are making. Often the very small leaves do not have covered leaf stems and rather than show the wire, it is best to bind them so close to the main stem that there is no visible leaf stem.

Examine the real flower, or pictures of one, to create the effect of the natural arrangement of stems and leaves. You will see that some seem to have leaves which appear to be coming straight out of the stem, as in the azalea, in which case these are always bound closely to the main stem.

Leaves are of so many different shapes and sizes, each with their own pattern of veins, that in order to simplify flower making we have given you here a few basic types. The first leaf shape shows a single terminal leaf and pairs of lateral leaves.

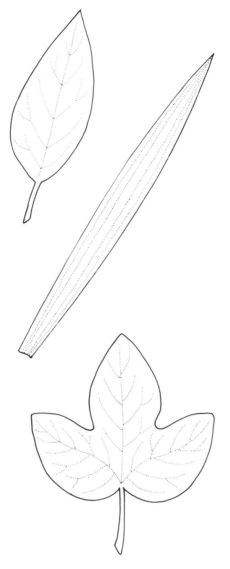

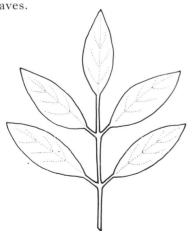

Stems

In flowercraft the main stem of the flower or plant is made from a piece of wire, the thickness of which depends on the size of the flower; for instance, a little violet would have a stem of No. 3 wire, a begonia or poinsettia would have a sturdier stem of No. 1 wire.

Fabric flower stems are generally covered with floral tape or green cotton fabric. Paper flower stems should be bound with crêpe paper. (See pages 13 and 16.)

If you wish to extend the main stem of a flower or give it a little support, you must attach it to something stronger like a stick or dowel rod. Place the top of the stick by the side of the stem so they overlap by about 5cm (2in.) and bind the two together with No. 3 wire. Wind a narrow strip of green crêpe paper or floral tape tightly round the join and continue winding down the stick to cover it, gluing the end of the strip in place.

You may wish to thicken the stem of your flower, especially if you are making a flower with a thick, fleshy stem, like a daffodil. To do this place the flower stem inside a drinking straw so that the straw comes up to the base of the flower. Dab glue on the flower base so that the straw sticks firmly to it. Then, starting from the base of the flower, wind a narrow strip of green crêpe paper down the straw to cover it, gluing the end of the strip in place.

There are several flowers in this book such as the magnolia and apple blossom, which can be assembled on a twig rather than a length of stem wire. Find an interestingly shaped twig with two or three branches. The flowers and leaves which you are going to attach to the twig should have stems of their own made of uncovered wire. Hold a flower at the end of a twig with its stem down the side of the twig and bind tightly with brown floral tape or crêpe paper strip to match the color of the twig. Continue winding down the stem, incorporating leaves in the same way. Repeat for the other branches on the twig. Berries can also be wired to these real twigs for a large arrangement.

When assembling a flower which has several buds, flowers and leaves attached to the same stem, take care to notice whether these are arranged in pairs opposite each other, or singly on alternate sides of the stem. Otherwise you may miss a distinctive feature of the character of the finished flower.

Single Flowers

On the following pages the instructions, patterns and ideas for using many different flowers with their foliage are given. Suggestions for the appropriate materials, whether paper or wax or different fabrics such as cotton, velvet silk or organza are given, but these suggestions should only be regarded as a guide. Once you have tried the simpler flowers, do not be afraid to experiment with wild and unusual colors and textures. There are countless possibilities and alternatives.

ROSE

This beautiful fabric rose will make a delightful decoration for a summer hat or give a touch of sophistication to an evening dress when worn as a corsage. If, however, you wish to use it in a flower arrangement, you will need to add a thicker stem. The center of the rose can be made in a different fabric from the petals.
For a paper rose, see page 12.

For a fabric rose you will need:
Satin, velvet, organza or silk which has been starched in chosen color for the petals
Green fabric for leaves
No. 1 and No. 3 wire
Stamens either from a hobby shop or made from sisal twine and dipped in yellow poster paint
Green floral tape
Knitting needle
Starch (in an aerosol can)
Quick-drying clear glue
Scissors
Wire cutters
Spoon
Foam rubber sponge

Step 1 To make the petals
Cut petal shapes out of selected fabric using patterns 1, 2 and 3. Make several for a large rose.
Pierce the center of each shape with a very sharp knitting needle.
Spray petals lightly with starch.
Cup each petal (see page 15) and then curl the petal edge over a heated knitting needle. (Use a salt-spoon to cup the smaller petals.)

Step 2 To assemble the flower
Cut a 30cm (12in.) length of No. 3 wire and fold it in half.
Make a small bud of cotton wool (cotton).
Place it at the bend of the folded wire, and twist the wire around it to bind tightly. Then bring down the ends of the wire together to form a stem.
Take the smallest petal shape, put the stem down through the center and push the petal up to the bud.

Put glue on each petal and fold over the bud with the petals overlapping to hide it.

Repeat with the second and third petal shapes, but put less glue on each petal.

If making a large rose continue attaching petal shapes, leaving the last petals to fall away from the rose by gluing only around the center of the flower.

Step 2a To assemble the flower with stamens

If you would prefer a rose with stamens, twist the 30cm (12in.) length of No. 3 wire round a bunch of stamens to secure, and bring down the ends to form a stem.

Cut a tiny slit in the center of the petal shapes to allow them to go round both stamens and stem.

Glue the petal shape at the base of the stamens and wrap around, allowing the stamen heads to show. Continue adding petals to build up the rose as above.

Step 3 To make the calyx

Cut shape from pattern 4 in green fabric.

Make a hole in the center and push it up the stem.

Put a little glue on the inner side of the calyx so that it sticks to the base of the flower.

Bind the calyx base and stem with floral tape.

Step 4 To make the leaves

Cut leaf shapes out of folded green fabric using pattern 5.

Cut lengths of No. 3 wire 2.5cm (1in.) longer than the leaves and bind with floral tape.

Glue one between two leaf shapes. Make three or five leaves to be arranged together on one leaf stem.

Cut a 12.5cm (5in.) length of No. 3 wire for the leaf stem.

Make one leaf the terminal leaf and bind it to the top of the leaf stem with floral tape.

Attach the lateral leaves in pairs as you continue to wind the tape down the stem.

Step 5 To assemble the flower and leaves

Twist the flower and leaf stems together and bind with floral tape. If you want a stronger stem, cut a piece of No. 1 wire to desired length. Twist the flower and leaf stems onto the main stem, bind the join and continue winding down the stem.

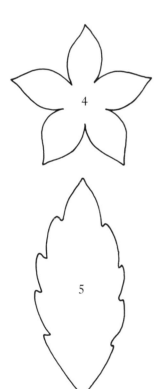

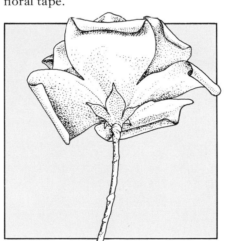

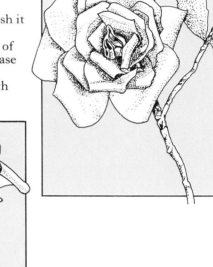

Right *A single exquisite specimen red rose can give a romantic and surprising touch to a gift, or indeed be a gift in itself. A bunch of deep red roses, still in bud, not yet full blown, is certainly original—and will last for more than a day!*

Below *This full blown silk rose with soft velvet leaves rests prettily on a cushion, defying anyone to sit on it—it is however a very decorative idea. Try several cushions scattered on a bed or sofa with flowers sewn onto them in carefully matching or contrasting colors. Flowers with wide open petals are most suitable.*

Right *Delicate pink and white rosebuds with velvet leaves have been secured in the hair with hairpins. The rosebuds are made of white organza streaked with colored ink, using a fine brush. If you don't want to use too many hairpins, twist the stems of the rosebuds around each other very slightly to make a chain. This will then make them feel much more secure in your hair. If you wish to wear a single rosebud only, simply twist the binding wire round the loop in the hairpin, and slide the pin into your hair. The wristlet of rosebuds is made by twisting the stem of one of the flowers around the stems of the others to hold them in a bunch without using more wire. Stitch the flowers to a piece of ribbon and tie it in a bow around the wrist.*

Inset *These glamorous rosebud earrings are made from cotton fabric. After the calyx has been attached and firmly secured with glue, wind around the base once with a strip of green cotton fabric and glue again. The two ends of the No. 3 wire which would form its stem can then be cut off just below the calyx and bent over together to form a neat hook. This can then be attached to the hook of an earring clip. (See also page 72)*

Left *This simple bouquet of pink rosebuds is made from paper which has been tinted in shades of pink and white.*

ROSEBUD

The fabric for the rosebud can be treated to give some interesting effects. For instance it can be tinted by using ink and a fine brush or it can be dipped in dye solution, wrung out and allowed to dry which gives it a natural look. The rosebud can also be made in paper.

For a fabric rosebud you will need:
Silk, cotton fabric or organza which has been stiffened with starch for petals
Suggested colors: pink, white, lemon, peach, red
Soft green fabric for sepal and leaves
Matching green bias binding or a strip of the green fabric cut on the bias
No. 3 wire
Cotton wool (cotton)
Knitting needle
Starch (in an aerosol can)
Quick-drying clear glue
Scissors
Wire cutters

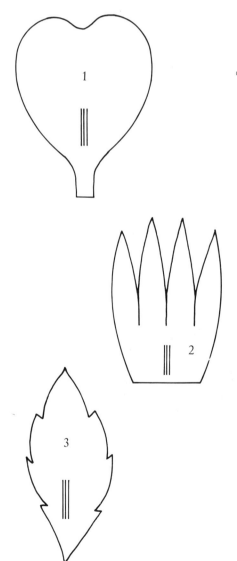

Step 1 To make the bud
Cut out three bud shapes from pattern 1 and spray with starch. Leave a knitting needle standing in hot water for a few minutes, take out and dry. Use to curl the edges of the petals as shown.
Cut a 20cm (8in.) length of No. 3 wire and fold in half.
Make a small bud of cotton wool (cotton) and glue onto the bend of the folded wire.

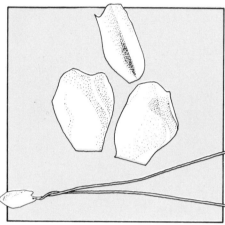

Dab glue on one side of a petal shape and wrap it around the cotton bud to cover it completely.
Dab glue on the second petal shape at the base only and wrap around the first petal shape less tightly.

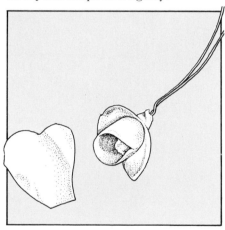

Repeat with the third petal.
Dab glue around the base of the petals and wrap with cotton wool (cotton) to form a calyx.
Cut out sepals from pattern 2 and glue around the calyx.
Attach matching green bias binding or strip of fabric to base of sepals and wind neatly down the rest of the stem.

Step 2 To make the leaves
For this dainty little bud cut leaves from a single thickness of fabric. Cut three leaf shapes from pattern 3. Cut a length of No. 3 wire for each leaf 2.5cm (1in.) longer than the length of the leaf.
Glue wires, uncovered, down the backs of the leaves.

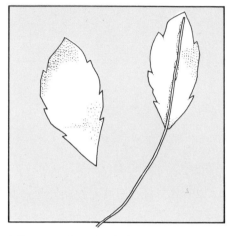

Three or five single leaves grow on one leaf stem.
Cut a 13cm (5in.) length of No. 3 wire for the leaf stem.
Cut a very thin strip of matching green fabric (if this fabric has been sized or starched it will not fray). Take one leaf as the terminal leaf and begin to bind the leaf stem onto the main stem, using the fabric strip. Attach the lateral leaves as you wind down. Put them opposite each other and, holding them in place, bind the stems together. Use glue if necessary to secure.

Step 3 Finishing touches
Twist the base of the bud and leaf stems together.
Bend the leaf back from the flower stem.

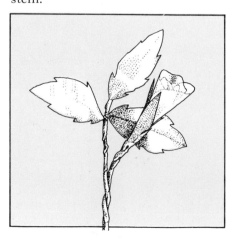

POPPY

This large paper poppy is easy to make and looks very realistic. It is different from the fabric poppy described on page 14, as it is the large cultivated variety.

For a paper poppy you will need:
Prepared red crêpe paper for petals
Black and green crêpe paper
No. 1 and No. 3 wire
Wire cutters
Quick-drying clear glue
Scissors
Black pastel

Step 1 To make the petals

Cut out four petals in red crêpe paper using pattern 1.
Shade each petal along the grain from its base to just above the center part with black pastel. This is to give the dusty black effect of pollen. Stretch each petal slightly across its width just below the center so that the top of the petal curves inwards.

Step 2 To make the stamens and center

Take a piece of scrap black paper and roll into a ball about the size of a large pea or marble.
Cover this with a 7.5cm (3in.) square of black crêpe paper, with the silkier side of the paper on the outside. Stretch this square over and around the ball and twist the ends together at the bottom.
Cut a piece of black crêpe paper 17.5cm (7in.) long across the grain of the paper and 8.5cm (3½in.) wide and stretch slightly along its length. Cut a fringe to half its depth, making sure that the grain of the paper runs down the strands of the fringe.
Twist the ends of the fringe between your finger and thumb to make the stamens.
Gather the stamens around the ball and secure at base with No. 3 wire.

Step 3 To assemble the flower

Arrange the first two petals opposite each other around the stamen center.

Add the other two petals opposite each other in the remaining spaces. Bind the base of the petals securely with No. 3 wire.
Cut a length of No. 1 wire for the main stem up to 30cm (12in.) long and make a small hook at one end. Push this down through the flower center to one side of the paper ball, so that the hook remains embedded in the base.
Cover the flower base and stem with a strip of green crêpe paper.

Step 4 To make a leaf

If you wish to make a leaf for this poppy, use the template for the fabric poppy leaf, enlarged if desired.
Cut out two leaf shapes from green crêpe paper and glue covered No. 3 wire, 5cm (2in.) longer than the leaf, between them.
Mark veins on the leaf with a scissor-blade.
Twist the leaf stem onto the main stem and cover join with green crêpe paper strip, winding it down to the end of the stem.

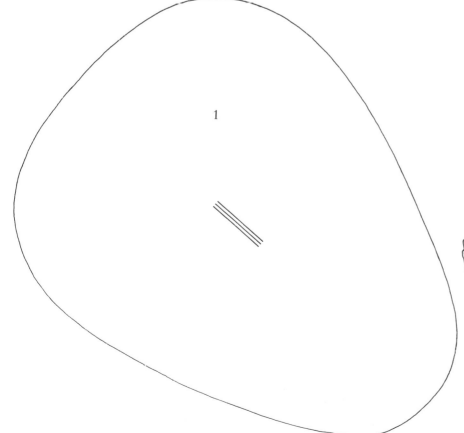

1

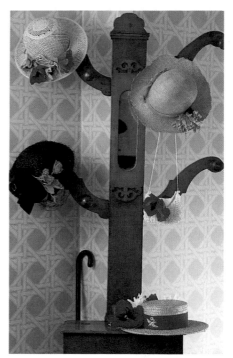

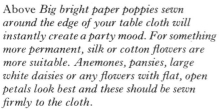

Above *Big bright paper poppies sewn around the edge of your table cloth will instantly create a party mood. For something more permanent, silk or cotton flowers are more suitable. Anemones, pansies, large white daisies or any flowers with flat, open petals look best and these should be sewn firmly to the cloth.*

Left *A girdle of bright poppies for a festive party mood. The poppy heads with their stems cut short can be twisted around a colorful belt or girdle to match or contrast with your dress. Or the long poppy stems can be twisted around each other to form the girdle and smaller flowers, such as daisies, can be attached between them.*

Right *Poppies and cornflowers in cotton fabric—the poppies bright sunshine colors, the cornflowers blue.*

Above *No need to buy a new hat—simply change the flowers which trim it! This is a much cheaper and very effective way of dressing up a straw hat. An old felt beret too might be given a new lease of life with a trimming of velvet sweet peas or violets. Flowers to be used in this way are best made with No. 3 wire only and sewn to the hat.*

Below left *The translucent sheen of a waxed anemone gives it the appearance of colored glass. This vase of waxed anemones makes an unusual ornament which will last for years. The simplicity of the flowers is emphasized in an uncluttered modern setting using glass and chrome, or with a dramatic décor of white and black.*

Below *Paper anemones made from prepared crêpe paper add a splash of color in a simple white vase.*

ANEMONE

The anemone is similar to the poppy but has more petals. It can be made in silk or fine cotton with a centre of black fabric covering a ball of cotton wool (cotton) surrounded by stamens of sisal twine dipped in black ink.

For a paper anemone you will need:
Prepared crêpe paper in chosen color for petals
Suggested colors: mauve, red, pink, white, heliotrope
Black and green crêpe paper
No. 1 and No. 3 wire
Quick-drying clear glue
Scissors
Wire cutters

Step 1 To make the petals
Cut eight petal shapes from pattern 1 in chosen color of crêpe paper.
Cup each petal across its broadest part.

Step 2 To make the stamen center
Take a small piece of scrap paper and roll into a ball about the size of a pea.
Cover this with a 3.5cm (1½in.) square of black crêpe paper, with the silkier side of the paper on the outside.
Stretch the paper over and around the ball and twist the ends together at the bottom.
Cut a strip of black crêpe paper 7.5cm (3in.) long, across the grain of the paper, and 3.5cm (1½in.) wide and stretch slightly along its length.
Cut a fine fringe to half the depth, making sure that the grain of the paper runs down the strands of the fringe.
Twist the ends of the fringe between your finger and thumb to make the stamens.
Gather the stamens around the center ball and secure at base with No. 3 wire.

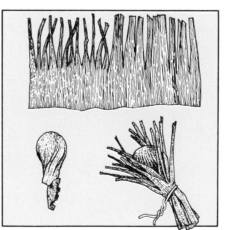

Step 3 To assemble the flower
Arrange the petals evenly around the stamen center.
Cut a 15cm (6in.) length of No. 3 wire.
Place the flower base in the center of the wire and twist it around to secure; bring the two ends down together.

Open out the petals to reveal the stamen center.
Cut a length of No. 1 wire for the main stem 20cm (8in.) long and make a very small hook at one end.
Push this down through the flower center so that the hook remains embedded in the base.
Twist the No. 3 and No. 1 wires together.
Cover the flower base and stem with a strip of green crêpe paper.

Step 4 To make the stem foliage
Cut two foliage strips from pattern 2 in green crêpe paper.
Glue one around the flower base as sepals and the other 3.5cm (1½in.) lower down the stem.

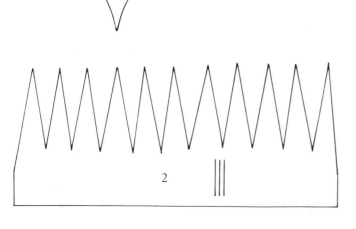

1

2

DAISIES

Marguerite daisy

This daisy can be made to look bright and cheerful with colored petals: try orange or shades of red and blue.

For a paper marguerite daisy you will need:
White crêpe paper for petals
Yellow and green crêpe paper
No. 1 and No. 3 wire
Quick-drying clear glue
Scissors
Wire cutters

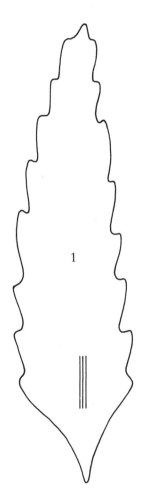

Step 1 To make the petals
From a roll of white crêpe paper, cut off a piece 8.5cm (3½in.) wide. When opened out it should be 40cm (16in.) long.
Fold in half and fold in half again lengthwise to make four thicknesses. Draw ten petal shapes freehand as shown, the petals ending halfway down the strip, and cut out.

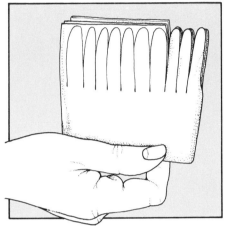

Unfold the petal strip; you should have 40 petals.
Curl each of the petals slightly.

Step 2 To make the flower center
Take a strip of yellow crêpe paper 20cm (8in.) long and 10cm (4in.) wide. Stretch slightly along its length.
Fold over in half lengthways to a depth of 5cm (2in.) without making a sharp crease at the fold.

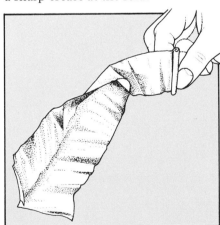

Roll up this folded strip tightly and glue the end to hold the roll together. The spiral top forms the flower center.

Step 3 To assemble the flower
Hold the yellow center in one hand, then take the long petal strip, and with the curls facing away from you, pleat it around the center to form a large white daisy.

Step 4 To make the stem
Cut a 25cm (10in.) length of No. 1 wire for stem.
Make a small hook at one end and place at the side of the yellow center; pull downwards so the hook is embedded and wrap the base firmly with No. 3 wire.
Cover base and stem with a strip of green crêpe paper.

Step 5 To make the leaves
For each leaf, cut out two shapes from pattern 1 in green crêpe paper.
Cut a piece of No. 3 wire 2.5cm (1in.) longer than the leaf.
Bind with green crêpe paper and glue wire between two leaf shapes.
Position leaves in pairs opposite each other, halfway down the stem, binding the leaf stems to the flower stem with No. 3 wire.
Cover with green crêpe paper.

Step 6 Finishing touches
Open the petals out away from the flower center to make a flat flower head.
This daisy can, of course, be made smaller or larger by increasing or decreasing the width of the white paper cut from the roll and making a larger or smaller center.

Above *A daisy chain makes a charming necklace and bracelet—and so easy to do too! Just twist the stems of several small field daisies together. A single small daisy attached to a hair grip with some fine No. 3 wire will also look very pretty in the hair.*

Above right *These large marguerite daisies are some of the most effective flowers to make—they blend so well with other flowers, their crisp whiteness acting as a foil for other colors. They also look very attractive on their own or with real greenery in a simple vase.*

Right *A bedspread edged with country flowers—daisies, poppies and cornflowers. Fabric flowers are most suitable for this and can be sewn around the hem.*

Above *Bunches of paper cornflowers make an original, if simple, decoration tied with ribbon and hung upside down like dried flowers.*

Below *Pink and blue cornflowers made from paper go well together with heather or statice—and there is no need to make many of them to fill a vase with such an arrangement. Dried flowers, of course, need no water and with the paper ones will give you an everlasting arrangement with good contrasting textures.*

For a fabric marguerite daisy you will need:
Starched white cotton fabric for petals
Yellow velvet or scrap material for the center
No. 1 and No. 3 wire
Green floral tape

Step 1 To make the petals
Cut a strip of cotton fabric 5cm (2in.) wide and 30cm (12in.) long.
Fold in half and fold in half again to make four thicknesses of fabric.
Draw ten petal shapes as for the paper marguerite.
Cut out petal shapes and unfold the strip of petals.

Step 2 To make the fabric flower center
Use a 7.5cm (3in.) square of bright yellow velvet.
Roll up a small ball of scrap paper or fabric the size of an ordinary marble.
Cover this with velvet and secure with No. 3 wire.

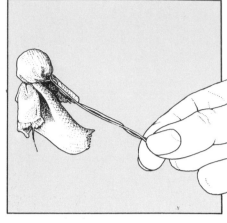

Step 3 To assemble the flower
Assemble the fabric flower as for the paper marguerite.

Step 4 To make the stem
Using a 25cm (10in.) length of No. 1 wire, hooked 1cm ($\frac{1}{2}$in.) from the end, insert down the side of the flower center and bind with floral tape.

Field daisy

The small field or common daisy is made in the same way as the marguerite, but is simpler and smaller with a different stem.

For a paper field daisy you will need:
The same materials as for the marguerite daisy, but use No. 3 wire for stem and No. 4 wire for binding.

Step 1 To make the petals
Take one strip of white crêpe paper 15cm (6in.) long and 3.5cm (1$\frac{1}{2}$in.) wide.
Fold in half and then fold in half again to give four thicknesses.
Cut out several long narrow petals with rounded edges halfway down the strip.

Step 2 To make the flower center
Take a small strip of yellow paper 2.5cm (1in.) wide by 10cm (4in.) long.
Roll it up tightly and glue the end to hold the roll together.

Step 3 To assemble the flower
Pleat the strip of white petals around the spiral flower center and secure with No. 4 wire.

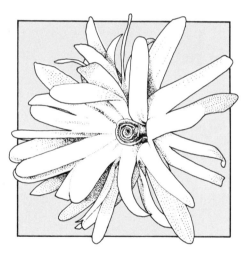

Step 4 To make the stem
This small daisy does not need a strong stem.
Cut a 25cm (10in.) length of No. 3 wire.
Place the flower base in the center of the wire and twist wire around it, bringing the two ends down together to make a stem.
Cover with a very narrow strip of green crêpe paper.

CORNFLOWER

The cornflower looks very natural when made of paper, but it can also be made in a fine cotton which has been starched. A posy of purple, blue, pink and white cornflowers can be charming.

For a paper cornflower you will need:
Blue crêpe paper for petals
Leaf green crêpe paper
No. 2 and No. 3 wire
Quick-drying clear glue
Scissors
Wire cutters
Pinking shears

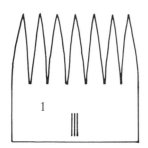

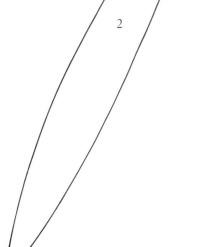

Step 1 To make the flower
Cut a 3.5cm (1½in.) wide strip 30cm (12in.) long in blue crêpe paper. Fold into four and cut along one length with pinking shears.
Cut down 2.5cm (1in.) between the V-shapes to make a fringe.

Gather this strip up to make a flower head and bind at base with No. 3 wire.
Cut a 20cm (8in.) length of No. 2 stem wire and make a small hook at one end.
Push the wire down the center of the flower so that the hook remains embedded in the flower base.
Twist binding wire onto the stem.

Step 2 To make the sepal
Cut a small sepal shape from pattern 1 in green crêpe paper and glue around the base of the flower.
Curl the points of the sepal out and away from the flower head.

Step 3 To make the leaf
The leaf is cut from a double-thickness of green crêpe paper using pattern 2.
Cut a piece of No. 3 wire 2.5cm (1in.) longer than leaf.
Glue the uncovered wire down the center and between the leaf shapes.
Make two leaves to a flower stem and attach alternately down the stem, opposite each other.
Bind stem with a green crêpe paper strip.
Bend leaves back and away from the stem.

Above *A big bold peony can be attached to the end of a plait by using No. 2 wire to secure it around the plait or to a ribbon which can then be tied around the hair. Smaller flowers are arranged in the plait, secured by their short wire stems.*

Right *Peonies, from palest pink to deep cerise, mixed with daisies, poppies and anemones, make a colorful Hawaiian garland for a party or a carnival. This garland is made entirely from paper flowers which will retain their crisp and fresh quality long after the party is over. The stems of the larger flowers are twisted around each other to make up a long necklace, and the smaller flowers, with shorter, finer stems are then twisted in between them. A softer and more flowing garland could be made from fabric flowers bound to a cord or ribbon with their No. 3 wire stems and then stitched to secure them in place. The garland is most effective if a lot of flowers are used, placed very close to each other, but facing in different directions so that they can be viewed from all angles.*

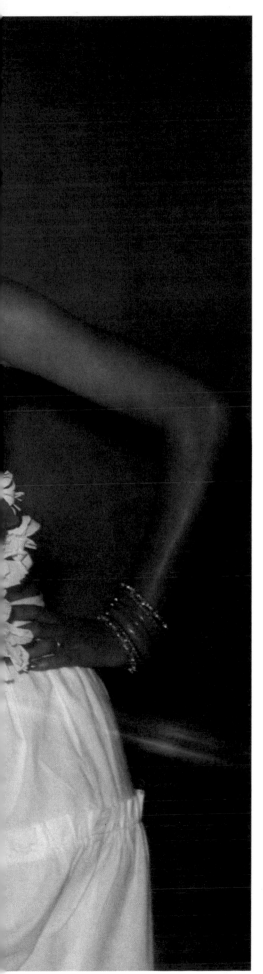

Above *These small white peonies made from crêpe paper delicately tinted with palest pink are mixed with real laurel leaves and heather to form a long garland which can decorate a staircase on special occasions, such as a wedding. The flowers and leaves are stuck into a long roll of wire netting which can then be bent to the desired shape. The garland is attached to the staircase with wire and fine string. The peonies do not need their strong stems for this garland. Simply attach the flower heads by the No. 3 wire used to bind their bases. (See page 158.)*

Left *A gift box can be made much more fun when topped with a large paper peony looking like an exotic pompon.*

PEONY

This is an easy flower to make. It can be made from plain pink, white or red crêpe paper, but the effect is enhanced if the paper is prepared and tinted beforehand. A mixture of pink, white and mauve colors in crêpe paper will also give an attractive colorful effect.

For a paper peony you will need:
Crêpe paper in chosen color(s) for petals
Green crêpe paper
No. 1 and No. 3 wire
Sisal twine
Quick-drying clear glue
Scissors
Wire cutters

Step 1 To make the petals
Cut a 10cm (4in.) piece from a folded roll of crêpe paper (tinted and dried, if desired).
Draw a three-petal shape onto the folded paper and cut out.

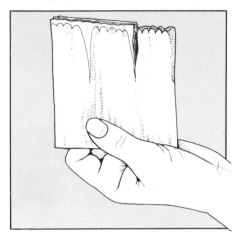

This gives a series of petal shapes when you open up the strip which should be 120cm (4ft) in length. For a smaller flower, simply use a shorter piece of paper.
Cup each petal.

Step 2 To make the stamens
Cut a 7.5cm (3in.) piece of sisal twine, and separate the strands at one end. These can be dipped in yellow poster paint, if desired.

Step 3 To assemble the flower
Place the bunch of stamens at one end of the petal strip so that the tops are 2.5cm (1in.) below the petal tips. Gather the strip of petals around the stamens and bind the base of the flower with No. 3 wire.

Cut a 20cm (8in.) piece of No. 1 wire for stem and make a hook at one end. Push through the flower head so that the hook remains embedded in the calyx.
Cover calyx and stem with green crêpe paper strip.

RHODODENDRON

Seven to ten individual florets will make a full rhododendron flower. The leaves are varnished to make them dark and shiny.

For a paper rhododendron you will need:
Crêpe paper for petals
Suggested colors: red, pink, white, mauve or heliotrope
White and dark green crêpe paper
No. 1 and No. 3 wire
Quick-drying clear glue
Scissors
Wire cutters
Varnish
Brown poster paint

Step 1 To make a floret
Cut petal shapes from pattern 1 in chosen color of crêpe paper.
For stamens, cut a strip of white crêpe paper 7.5cm (3in.) deep and 3.5cm (1½in.) wide.
Cut a fringe 5cm (2in.) deep.
Twist ends between your finger and thumb into long spirals.
Paint tips with dark brown poster paint, and mark one petal with dark brown dots.
Bunch together and twist around at base.
Glue petals in a crown shape and insert stamen bunch level with the tops of the petals.

Pinch in at base of petals and place in the center of a 15cm (6in.) length of No. 3 wire, twisting the wire around to secure. Pull the ends of the wire down together to form the floret stem.
Cover stem with green crêpe paper strip.

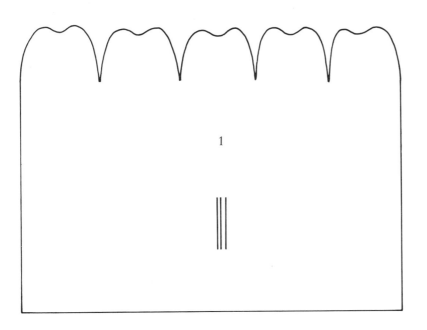

Step 4 To assemble the flower

Take seven to ten florets and twist their stems together at the base. Cut a 20cm (8in.) length of No. 1 wire and make a small hook at the end.

Place the hook of wire into the twisted floret stems and bind securely with No. 3 wire.

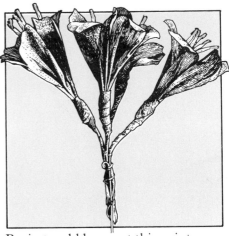

Begin to add leaves at this point, fairly close together around the stem. Bind main stem with a strip of brown crêpe paper, incorporating the larger leaves as you wind down. The leaves should show about 1cm ($\frac{1}{2}$in.) of their stems.

Step 2 Finishing touches for floret

Curl and stretch each petal with a scissor-blade so that it bends right back from the center to reveal the stamens.

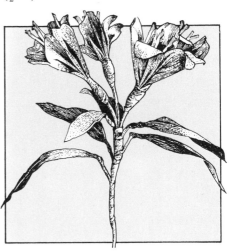

Step 3 To make the leaves

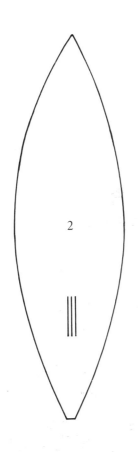

Cut several leaf shapes from a double-thickness of green crêpe paper using pattern 2.

Cut more pairs of leaves in increasing sizes using pattern 2 as a guide.

For each leaf cut a piece of No. 3 wire 2.5cm (1in.) longer than the leaf. Glue the uncovered wire between the two leaf shapes, then cover the leaf stem with a narrow strip of green crêpe paper.

Spray one side of each leaf with varnish.

Mark veins in the leaves with back of scissors.

Above *An unused fireplace, too pretty to be neglected, can become a focal point in the room once more, when filled with colorful rhododendrons.*

Left *Rhododendrons require considerable patience if you wish to make many of them —but the results are stunning. These paper rhododendrons are arranged in florist's foam at the bottom of this bowl. For this arrangement make eight large blooms with plenty of leaves which fill in the spaces between the flowers and set off their lovely colors.*

ORCHID

A single bloom can add an exotic touch to a hat or dress: for this you would need a shorter stem. It also looks splendid in a tall narrow-necked vase.

For a fabric orchid you will need:
Silk or velvet in shades of pale green, heliotrope or cream, for petals
No. 1 and No. 3 wire
One pipe cleaner for pistil
Yellow pastel
Floral tape, in green and the color of the petals
Felt-tip pen in a shade darker than the petals
Quick-drying clear glue
Scissors
Wire cutters

Step 1 To make the petals
There are three different types of petals. The petal for pattern 3 can be in a lighter or darker shade.
Cut three petals from pattern 1, two petals from pattern 2 and one large petal from pattern 3.
Using a felt-tip pen, mark the center of one side of the large petal with spots.
Cut five 15cm (6in.) lengths of No. 3 wire.
Bind each with colored floral tape.
Glue the wires along the length of the underside of each petal, except for the large petal.

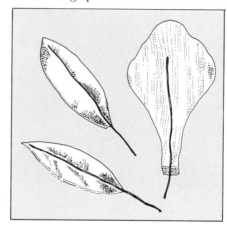

Step 2 To make the pistil
Use one pipe cleaner folded in half and twisted together.
Color it bright yellow with pastel.
Put a little glue on the base of the spotted side of the large petal.
Place the pistil on the glued surface and fold the large petal around the pistil, enclosing it.

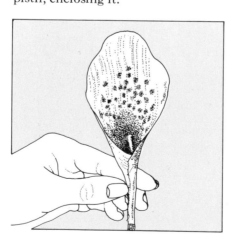

Step 3 To assemble the flower
Take up the two No. 2 petals and position them either side of a No. 1 petal.
Place the two remaining No. 1 petals so that they form the configuration of a star.

Finally, place the large petal between them and slightly above the lower No. 1 petals.
Cut a 30cm (12in.) length of No. 1 wire and make a 1cm ($\frac{1}{2}$in.) hook at the end.
Push this down through the center of the flower, so that the hook is embedded in the base.
Bind this stem with green floral tape.
Fold all the petals, except the large central one, out and down so that they curl slightly at the ends.

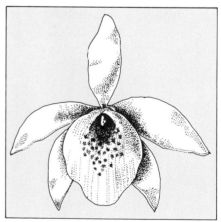

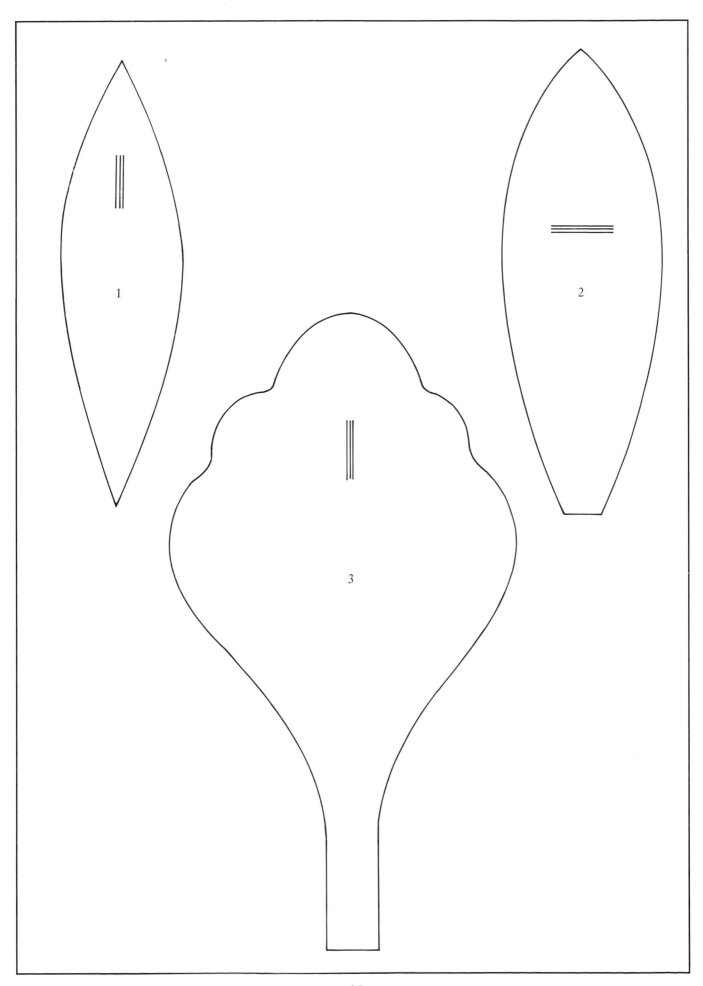

Above *Paper or fabric flowers are far better suited to the conditions of a shop window than real flowers, and seem to be much more in character with these stylized ladies. The orchids worn by the lady in the foreground are made from paper. Her friends are wearing arum lilies and roses. The basket is filled with white stephanotis.*

Left *This exotic silk orchid was made specially to match the silk dressing gown. They both certainly deserve to be seen, so let's hope they won't be alone for very long!*

Right *These paper orchids have been made from pink and white crêpe paper tinted together beforehand.*

For a paper orchid
This is made in a similar way to the fabric orchid, using the same patterns for the different petals.

You will need:
Crêpe paper for petals in the color of your choice
Green crêpe paper
No. 1 and No. 3 wire
One pipe cleaner or yellow crêpe paper for pistil
Felt-tip pen in a shade darker than the petals
Quick-drying clear glue
Scissors
Wire cutters

Step 1 To make the petals
The petals can be made in either a single or double-thickness of crêpe paper.
It is important when cutting out the petals to make sure the grain of the paper is going in the right direction as indicated on the patterns.
Cut three petals from pattern 1 and one large petal from pattern 3 with the grain of the paper running vertically (down their length).
Cut two petals from pattern 2 with the grain of the paper running horizontally (across their width).
Flute the sides of these two petals.
Using a felt-tip pen mark the center of one side of the large petal with spots.
Cut five 15cm (6in.) lengths of No. 3 wire.
Bind each with a crêpe paper strip in the same color as the petals.
Glue the wires along the underside of each petal, except for the large petal.
Curl back the sides of the lower part of the large petal, using a knitting needle.

Step 2 To make the pistil
Make as for fabric orchid using a pipe cleaner.
Or cut a 20cm (8in.) length of No. 3 wire and fold over four times so that it is 5cm (2in.) long. Twist together, leaving a loop at one end.
Bind with a narrow strip of yellow crêpe paper.

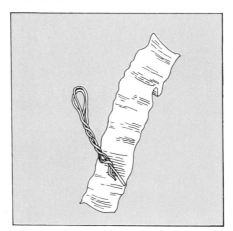

Put a little glue on the base of the spotted side of the large petal.
Place the pistil on the glued surface and fold the petal around the pistil, enclosing it.
The lower edges of the large petal should curl back slightly.

Step 3 To assemble the flower
Assemble as for the fabric orchid.

AZALEA

The azalea head is made up of approximately 12 florets. The flower is similar to the rhododendron but smaller. It can be made up as a pot plant in which case the flowers and leaves should be made smaller and the stems shorter.

For a paper azalea you will need:
Crêpe paper for petals, preferably tinted in shades of pink, red and yellow
Green crêpe paper
No. 1 and No. 3 wire
Quick-drying clear glue
Scissors
Wire cutters
Sisal twine or alternatively yellow crêpe paper for stamens
Yellow poster paint

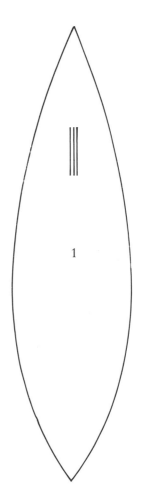

Step 1 To make individual florets
Cut a strip of paper 10cm (4in.) deep by 7.5cm (3in.) wide.
Fold to give five concertina folds.
Cut one end to a shallow point and open out the strip to give five petals.

Step 2 To make stamens
Cut a 3.5cm (1½in.) piece of twine and separate the strands at one end.

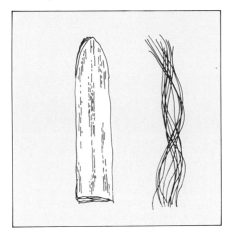

Dip this end in deep yellow poster paint, if desired.
Alternatively, make crêpe paper stamens from a strip of yellow paper 2.5cm (1in.) wide and 5cm (2in.) deep.
Cut a fringe halfway down and twist the ends between your finger and thumb for stamens.

Step 3 To assemble the florets to form the azalea head
Arrange each petal strip around a bunch of stamens.
Cut a 15cm (6in.) length of No. 3 wire.
Place the base of the floret in the center of the wire, twist the wire around and bring the ends down together to form a floret stem of about 7.5cm (3in.). The stamens should peep out from the bell of the flower.

Curl the petal tips outwards over a scissor-blade.
Bind stem with a strip of green crêpe paper.
Make 12 of these florets.
These are then joined at the base of the small stems to make one complete azalea flower.

Step 4 To make the leaves
The leaves form a star-like shape 2.5cm (1in.) below the flower.
Using pattern 1, cut out four leaves from a double-thickness of green crêpe paper (to make eight leaf shapes).
Cut a piece of No. 3 wire, 2.5cm (1in.) longer than the leaf, bind with green crêpe paper strip and glue between the leaf shapes.
Repeat for each leaf.
Spray with varnish for a dark and shiny effect.
If you are making small leaves for a potted plant make the leaf stem shorter, do not cover it and attach it close to the main plant stem.

Step 5 To assemble the whole flower and leaves
Cut a 30cm (12in.) piece of No. 1 wire, making a small hook at the end.
Twist the ends of the floret stems together and embed the wire hook in them.
Cut a 1cm (½in.) wide strip of green crêpe paper.
Put glue on the base of the florets, attach the crêpe paper and tightly bind the main stem 1cm (½in.) down.
Arrange the leaves in a star-like formation and bind to the stem with green crêpe paper strip.
Finish binding the stem with green crêpe paper.
If the flowers are to be used in a large arrangement their stems can be strengthened and lengthened by binding a strong twig to the stem with No. 3 wire and covering with green crêpe paper.

Above *A blaze of bright color from an azalea plant made in paper. The gently tinted effect is created by using shades of pink and red with white. The plant is at its best when the flowers are at different stages of opening, some fully open and others still in bud. The foliage too contributes to the final effect. A plant as large as this will take several hours to make but it will give you months of pleasure. What a beautiful gift it would be for someone!*

Right *Garlands of pale mauve as well as pink clematis, white stephanotis and pink apple blossom set the scene for a romantic summer evening party. The garlands are very quick and easy to make if you want to use paper flowers that you already have. Simply twist the wire stems around each other for this type of garland. In order to achieve a neater finish the whole length of the stems can then be bound with floral tape.*

Above *Paper flowers are ideal for restaurants and hotels—particularly if they are made much of for their own sake in a display and not used merely to fill a dark corner that doesn't get much light. Clearly they are marvellous for these corners too! The azaleas in this picture have had their stems lengthened (see also pages 142 and 158). The apple blossoms mixed in with the azaleas are bound to real twigs, which have been left uncovered.*

Right *This design for the* Clematis montana *flower was inspired by the wallpaper in this summery guest bedroom. It's one way of making sure that the most unexpected guests will always have flowers in their room.*

CLEMATIS

There are many varieties of clematis. Here we show you how to make the Montana variety which is a small, light pink flower that grows at the head of a long, trailing stem of pretty leaves. Several flowers can be joined together to make a garland.

For a paper clematis you will need:
Pink crêpe paper for petals
Green crêpe paper
No. 1 and No. 3 wire
Sisal twine
Quick-drying clear glue
Scissors
Wire cutters

Step 1 To make the flower
Cut a petal strip from pattern 1 in pink crêpe paper.
Cut a 5cm (2in.) length of sisal twine and open out and separate the strands at one end. It may need thinning out slightly as this is a small flower.
Cut a 15cm (6in.) length of No. 3 wire.
Wrap the petal strip around the sisal twine stamens and place in the center of the length of wire. Bind the flower base and then pull the ends of the wire down together to form flower stem.

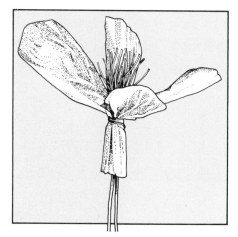

Step 2 To make the leaves
Each complete leaf has one terminal and two lateral leaves—all the same size and shape. Cut three single leaf shapes from pattern 2 in green crêpe paper.
Cut three pieces of No. 3 wire, one 17.5cm (7in.) long, the other two 7.5cm (3in.). Leave uncovered.

Glue the longer length of wire down the back of the terminal leaf and glue the smaller ones along the backs of the two lateral leaves on either side of the terminal leaf and twist their stems into the longer one.
Cover leaf stem with a strip of green crêpe paper.

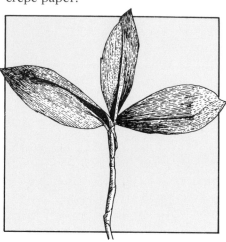

Step 3 To assemble the plant as a trailer
The leaves grow down the stem in pairs opposite each other with flowers at the top of the trailing stem.
Twist the leaf stems into the flower stem 5cm (2in.) down from the flower.
Bind a strip of green crêpe paper around the flower calyx and on down the stem to cover over where the leaves are joined.
At this point a piece of No. 1 wire can be added to form the main stem out of which other trailers can grow.
Add pairs of leaves at regular intervals down the stem. In this way you can add indefinitely to your trailing plant.

2

1

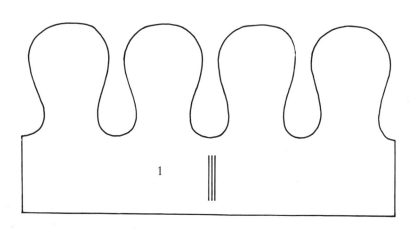

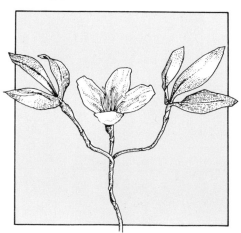

CARNATION

This flower is very rewarding and easy to make from good quality, soft, multi-layered paper napkins.

For a paper carnation you will need:
1 paper napkin in red, white, pink or yellow for petals
No. 1, No. 2 and No. 3 wire
Green crêpe paper
Quick-drying clear glue
Scissors
Pinking shears
Wire cutters

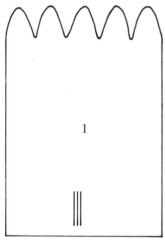

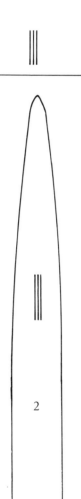

Step 1 To make the flower
Take a paper napkin folded in a square, and cut a piece 7.5cm (3in.) wide and 15cm (6in.) long from the square so that no folded edges remain.
Cut along each 15cm (6in.) edge with pinking shears.
Fold this rectangular piece in 1cm (½in.) concertina folds along its length.
Take a piece of No. 3 wire 30cm (12in.) long and bind it tightly round the center of the folded paper, bringing the two ends down together to form a stem.

Carefully separate each fine layer of tissue, bringing each one in towards the wired center as far as possible without tearing.
Do both sides in this way and the flower will then look like a carnation.

Step 2 To make the stem and calyx
Cut a 22.5cm (9in.) length of No. 1 stem wire and place alongside the No. 3 stem wire.
Bind the two together with more No. 3 wire.
Take a 2.5cm (1in.) strip, 15cm (6in.) long, of the same soft paper napkin and glue it around the base of the flower to form a base for the calyx.
Cut the calyx from pattern 1 in green crêpe paper.
Glue the calyx around the flower base.
Curl the calyx points over with scissors.
Bind the stem with a strip of green crêpe paper.

Step 3 To make the leaves
Using pattern 2, cut six leaf shapes from a double-thickness of green crêpe paper to make three leaves.
Cut three 15cm (6in.) lengths of No. 2 wire and glue between leaf shapes.
Curl the leaves over slightly at the tip.
Twist the leaf stems onto the main stem 5cm (2in.) below the flower and bind join and stem with crêpe paper.

Above *and* right *Carnations are so versatile —in fact they seem to be everywhere, sometimes where you wouldn't expect to find them! Pinks and carnations are made in exactly the same way except that a pink is approximately half the size of a carnation. Here, a pink is sewn to an elasticated garter covered in black satin.*

Left *Paper carnations made from paper table napkins are among some of the easiest and most attractive flowers to make. Here they are being used as a table decoration as well as a place name-tag for a luncheon party. The flower can then be used as a buttonhole by the guests and taken home as a pleasant memento of the occasion.*

Below *To decorate a pair of soft fabric evening shoes, stitch or glue a carnation onto each upper. Alternatively, stitch the flower to a circle of elastic which is worn, not too tightly, around the instep of the foot.*

LILIES

Madonna lily

This is a simple pretty flower which can be made in white or cream crêpe paper or in a fabric such as stiffened silk or velvet.

For a paper madonna lily you will need:
White crêpe paper for petals
Green crêpe paper
No. 1 and No. 3 wire
Six white pipe cleaners for stamens
Yellow and green pastels
Quick-drying clear glue
Scissors
Wire cutters

For patterns, see pages 66–7

Step 1 To make the petals
From white crêpe paper cut a piece 12.5cm (5in.) deep and 45cm (18in.) long.
Fold in half.
Place template from pattern 1 on folded paper and cut to make two identical shapes.
Make a double-thickness by joining these two shapes together at their points with a small dab of glue on each point.

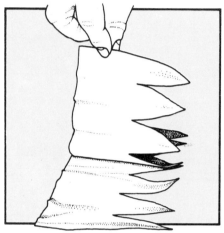

Lightly color one side with a yellow pastel from the center outwards, smudging the color into the points with your fingers.
Fold around to form a small crown with the yellow on the inside and glue the two edges together.

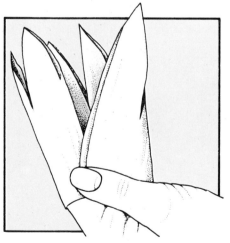

Step 2 To make the stamens
Take six white pipe cleaners and bend over the tops to form horizontal T-bars, each 1cm (½in.) long.
Holding all six together, color the T-bars bright yellow and the stamen stems soft green with pastel.

Step 3 To assemble the flower head
Cut a piece of No. 1 wire 30cm (12in.) long for the stem and make a hook 1cm (½in.) from the end.
Gather together the base of the flower and place the six pipe cleaners inside it so that the tips are level with the points of the petals.
Push the hooked stem wire down through the center of the flower, so that the hook is firmly embedded in the base of the flower.

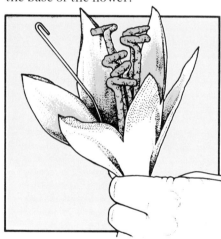

Wind No. 3 wire around the base to secure the flower, stamens and stem. Wind a green crêpe paper strip around the base of the flower and down the stem.

Step 4 Finishing touches for the flower head
Stretch each petal of the flower across its breadth and with a scissor-blade curl each petal away from the center of the flower.

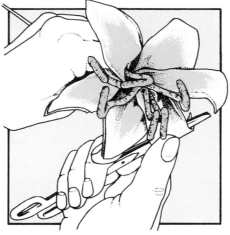

Step 5 To make the bud
Cut one square with sides of 12.5cm (5in.) in white crêpe paper. Color one side creamy yellow as for the lily flower and keep the colored side showing when you fold the bud. Fold the square in half diagonally, but do not crease the paper too firmly.

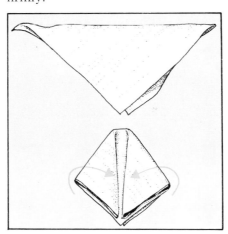

Bring the two points widest apart in towards each other and down to meet the third point. Repeat the action by folding the two points into the center and glue in place.
Cut a length of No. 1 wire 20–30cm (8–12in.) long with a 1cm (½in.) hook at the end.
Push the wire down through the bud until the hook catches at the base of the bud.

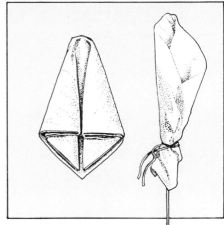

Bind the base with No. 3 wire to secure.
Cover stem and bud base with a green crêpe paper strip.

Step 6 To make the leaves
Cut the leaf shapes from pattern 2. For each leaf cut two leaf shapes in green crêpe paper.
Cut a piece of No. 3 wire 6cm (2½in.) longer than the leaf.
Glue two leaf shapes together, with the uncovered wire down the center. Make six to eight leaves.

Step 7 To assemble the flowers, buds and leaves
Several flowers and buds can be put together to give the appearance of a growing lily stem.
The buds are arranged at the top of the main stem above the flowers.
If the leaves are to be attached, bind them to the main stem in pairs and curl them over to look as natural as possible.
If a very strong and rigid stem is required, bind a twig to the stem wire with No. 3 wire and cover the join with a strip of green crêpe paper.
Bind everything together with a final strip of green crêpe paper.

Ideas for lilies

Right *Madonna lilies, with the flowers and buds bound together with the leaves on one strong wooden stem, make a beautiful and unusual bridal or evening bouquet. These lilies are made in paper, but the bouquet would look as good in cotton or silk.*

Left *Another single stem of madonna lilies, this time smaller with fewer flowers, makes a charmingly romantic decoration for a wedding gift. However practical the gift inside may be, the lily will serve as a beautiful reminder of the great day.*

Below *Lilies are particularly suitable for church decorations as this arrangement of arum and madonna lilies demonstrates. They have been put into a vase with florist's foam and the stems of the tallest flowers have been extended to give them more height. Real foliage has been used in addition to the paper lily leaves.*

Tiger lily

The tiger lily is distinguished by its markings and open petals. It is made here in a creamy white fabric, but shades of gold, orange, brown and yellow can also be used, with the markings and stamen ends in a darker tone.

For a fabric tiger lily you will need:
Heavy satin that has been stiffened for petals
Crêpe paper for stamen ends in a darker shade than the chosen petal fabric
No. 1 and No. 3 wire
Green floral tape
Green thread-covered wire for stamens
Felt-tip pen in a shade to match stamen ends
Quick-drying clear glue
Scissors
Wire cutters

For patterns, see pages 66–7

Step 1 To make the flower
Cut out six petals from pattern 3 using template.
Cut six pieces of No. 3 wire, each 2.5cm (1in.) longer than the petals. Glue one down the center of each petal.
Using a felt-tip pen, mark each petal with a background of shaded color and with dashes and dots to give a speckled effect, the background color and dots graduating from a mass near the base of the petals to none at all at the petal tips.

Step 2 To make the stamens
These can be made with No. 3 wire and floral tape instead of green thread-covered wire.
Each stamen is 12.5cm (5in.) long.
Cut a 1cm (½in.) square of crêpe paper for the stamen end.
Dab it with glue and fold in half.
Bend the thread-covered wire 1cm (½in.) at the end.
Fold the colored square over the wire, gluing it in place.
Repeat to make six stamens.

Step 3 To assemble the flower head
Cut a piece of No. 1 wire 25cm (10in.) long for the stem and hook the end.
Arrange the six petals and the six stamens evenly.
Push the stem wire down through the flower head so that the hook is embedded in the base.
Secure the base of the flower with No. 3 wire and cover with floral tape.
Continue winding the floral tape down to the end of the stem.

Step 4 Finishing touches
Curl the petals away from the center, leaving the stamens standing free.

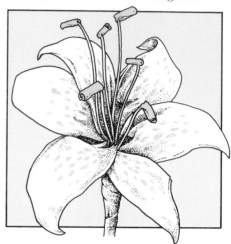

For a paper tiger lily
Make as the madonna lily in white crêpe paper, using a light pink pastel to color the inside.
Mark the petals with dark pink dashes and dots.
Use the same color for the stamen ends.
Try other color combinations too, like orange and dark brown.
Open out the petals to reveal the characteristic tiger lily markings.

Arum lily

This is the easiest of the lilies to make. It looks especially lovely when made out of white velvet. Color the velvet with pastel as for the paper lily and curl the petal back over a heated knitting needle. The paper arum lily can be waxed to give it a sheen.

For a paper arum lily you will need:
White crêpe paper for petals
Green crêpe paper
Two white pipe cleaners for each flower (or orange crêpe paper)
No. 1 and No. 3 wire
Yellow and orange pastels
Quick-drying clear glue
Scissors
Wire cutters
Clear varnish

For patterns, see pages 66–7

Step 1 To make the petals
Cut out two petal shapes in white crêpe paper, following pattern 4.
Glue them together to give a double-thickness of paper.
Shade one side of the paper lightly with soft yellow pastel and rub in the color with your finger to give a smooth effect.
Fold the sides inwards and glue the edges to make a trumpet shape, with the colored side inside.

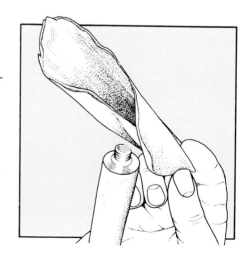

Step 2 To make the pistil

This can be made two ways.
Twist two pipe cleaners around each other to form a single stem and color it bright yellow with pastel. Then turn top over 1cm ($\frac{1}{2}$in.). Or double over a piece of No. 3 wire to a length of 15cm (6in.), leaving an open loop at the bend. Cover in orange crêpe paper, so that the loop in the wire forms a slightly thicker top end.

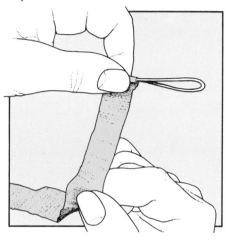

Step 3 To assemble a single flower

Cut a 25cm (10in.) length of No. 1 wire for the stem and bend the end over 1cm ($\frac{1}{2}$in.) from the top to form a hook.
Place the long end of the pistil in the flower and then pull the stem wire through, leaving the hook embedded in the base of the flower. Holding the pistil in position, bind the base of the flower, pistil and stem with No. 3 wire.

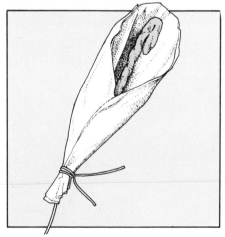

Wind base of flower and stem with a green crêpe paper strip.

Step 4 Finishing touches for the flower

Use both thumbs to stretch the flower widthways.
Bend the tip backwards to reveal the pistil.

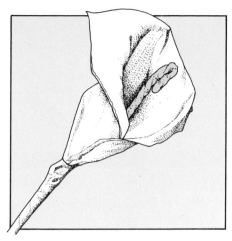

Step 5 To make the bud

Make the arum lily bud in the same way as the madonna lily bud.

Step 6 To make the leaf

Cut out two leaf shapes from pattern 5 in green crêpe paper. Make sure the grain of the paper runs across the width of the leaf.
Bind a 30cm (12in.) length of No. 1 wire with green crêpe paper.
Dab glue lightly around the edge and down the center of one leaf shape.
Place the covered wire down the center of the leaf and lay the other leaf directly on top, making sure they are glued firmly together.
Using both thumbs stretch the sides of the leaf out to flute the edges and curl gently around a knitting needle.

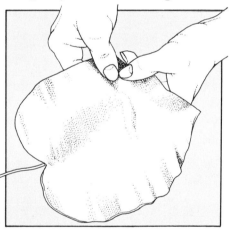

Use the knitting needle to make veins.
Varnish the top side to give a shiny appearance.

Step 7 To assemble the flower, bud and leaf

Attach the bud stem and leaf to the main flower stem and bind together with No. 3 wire.
Cover with a strip of green crêpe paper glued in place.

Above *and left Tiger lilies, immediately recognizable by their speckled petals and bold markings, are made from creamy-white silk which has been stiffened and then colored with a felt-tip pen. In this setting they have a delicate appearance, but they can be very dramatic when made in shades of orange or gold with dark brown markings. Tiger lilies can also be made in crêpe paper and look exotic in a tall art nouveau vase.*

Right *Arum lilies are striking flowers and can be made easily and quickly from crêpe paper. They look their best on their own or in an arrangement with other lilies. Try making them in creamy-white velvet too.*

Water lily

The water lily is most effective when waxed. Make the three layers of petals in various shades of pink, or experiment with more outrageous color combinations. For display, place the flower on a bed of two or three leaves.

For a paper water lily you will need:
Double-sided crêpe paper—one side yellow, one side white.
Green crêpe paper
No. 1 and No. 3 wire
Sisal twine
Clear varnish

For leaf pattern, see pages 66–7

Step 1 To make the stamens
Cut a piece of sisal twine 3.5cm (1½in.) long and separate the strands at one end.
Bind with No. 3 wire.
Dip ends in yellow poster paint.

Step 2 To make the petals
There are three kinds of petals: inner, middle and outer.
Inner petals Cut a 7.5cm (3in.) wide strip of double-sided crêpe paper 40cm (16in.) long. Fold over to make eight thicknesses.
Cut out six narrow pointed petals from the folded paper.
Open out the petal strip.
With the light side of the paper facing you, curl the petal tips inwards over a scissor-blade.
Middle petals Take a double-sided piece of crêpe paper 11.5cm (4½in.) deep and 50cm (20in.) long and fold in 3.5cm (1½in.) concertina folds.
Make a petal shape by cutting one end of the folded paper to a blunt point.
Open out the strip.
Outer petals Take a piece of double-sided paper 13.5cm (5½in.) deep and 41cm (16½in.) long, fold into 5cm (2in.) concertina folds.
Cut one end of the folded paper to a blunt point.
Open out petal strips.

Step 3 To assemble the flower
Take up the inner petal strip and gather it around the stamens with the petals curling inwards.
Bind base with No. 3 wire.
Take up middle petal strip and cup each petal.
With the lighter side of the paper on the inside, wind around the inner petals.
Secure the base with No. 3 wire.
Take up the outer petal strip and gather it around the flower.

Bind base of flower petals with No. 3 wire. Pull down the outer layer of petals so that they are as flat as they would be lying on the surface of the water.

Step 4 To form the calyx
Take a 2.5cm (1in.) wide strip of green crêpe paper to cover the bulky flower base and stamen stem which forms the short flower stem.

Step 5 To make the leaves
To make the water lily leaf follow instructions for the arum lily leaf, but make it slightly broader.
Curl the edges upwards with a knitting needle.
Spray the upper surface of the leaf with varnish to make it dark and shiny.
Make two or three leaves for each flower.
Leaves are not usually attached to the flower, but arranged around it.

Step 6 To wax the water lily flower and leaves
Melt two cupfuls of wax in a can placed in a saucepan of water (see page 17).
Wax the leaves by dipping each one separately into the wax.
Shake gently to loosen any drops of wax.
Set aside to dry.

Above *Paper water lilies on a bed of water lily leaves make an amusing setting for these playful china frogs. Sitting on the leaves they look very contented. The display has been arranged on a glass shelf.*

Right *Waxed water lilies are what is needed to brighten up this rather clinical, tiled bath surround. Take care not to splash them too much or you'll find that they quickly lose their color!*

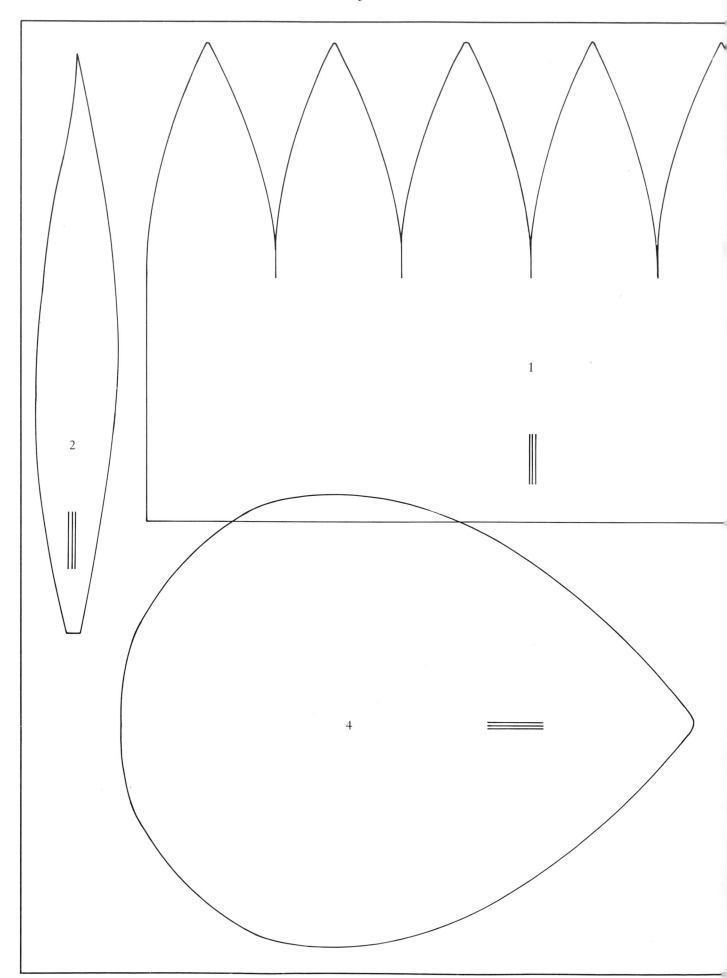

Patterns for madonna, tiger and arum lilies

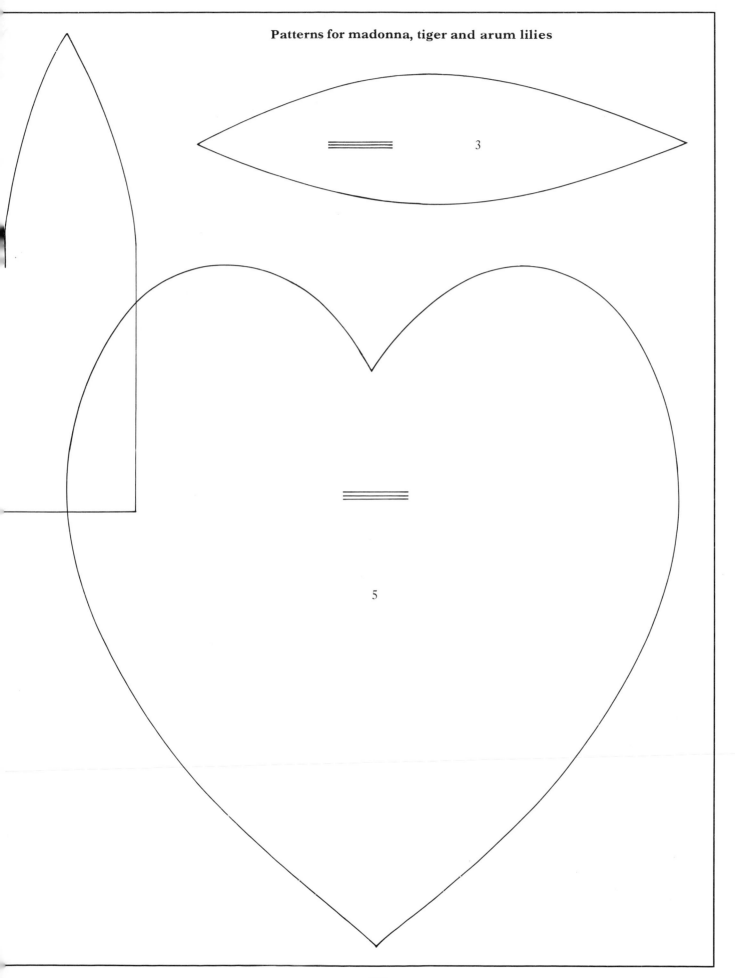

3

5

Top *Greetings cards or old photographs have a nostalgic charm when decorated with small violet heads and leaves. These can be fixed with glue onto the card without their wire stems. Trim the stamen stems if they show. The posy is made up of delicate waxed wild violets.*

Above left *The simple violet can be very pretty used to decorate individual place settings at a dining table or on a breakfast tray. Napkin rings can be decorated with flowers fixed onto them for a special occasion; use clear double-sided tape or quick-drying glue.*

Right *African violets can be used as single flowers in a vase or to decorate gifts and cards, as well as potted as a growing plant. Their flowers have more open petals than those of the wild violet and this makes them suitable for decorating tray cloths (attach with a few stitches) or displays of small flower heads as on page 72. For instructions for African violets, see page 117.*

A simple and romantic **spray of wild violets** made from cotton fabric is used here with a veil as a hat or head-dress.

You will need:
Six to eight fabric flowers
No. 3 wire
Green floral tape

The stem to the spray will be less bulky if the flower stems are left uncovered before twisting together. Arrange the flowers as desired. Twist the base of the stems around each other and secure by winding No. 3 wire around them. Cover the wire with floral tape as tightly and neatly as possible and continue binding all the way down the stems.

The piece of net is simply gathered together and lightly stitched to hold the gathers in place. The spray of violets is either stitched to the net or firmly held in place with large hairpins.

A **hair comb** decorated with small violets is very easy to make. Use the petals and leaves of the African violet but make them smaller with a single stamen. Simply arrange the tiny flowers and leaves as desired and either glue them directly onto the comb, or attach them first to a piece of thin cardboard cut to the shape of the top of the comb and then glue this to the comb itself.

VIOLETS

The simple violet

These instructions show how to make paper violets. The method for making a violet from fabric such as cotton, organza or velvet is the same, using fabric which has been stiffened with size or starch for the petals.

For a paper violet you will need:
Crêpe paper for petals in dark heliotrope or color of your choice
No. 3 and No. 5 wire
Single yellow stamens from a hobby shop
Wire cutters or pliers
Green floral tape
Small scissors
Quick-drying clear glue

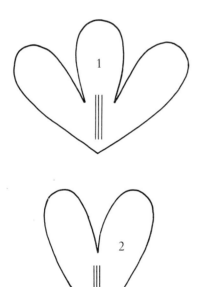

Step 1 To make the petals
Using patterns 1 and 2, cut out petal shapes from the dark heliotrope crêpe paper.

Step 2 To make the stem with a stamen
Cut a piece 10cm (4in.) in length from No. 3 stem wire.
Using wire cutters or pliers, twist the end of the wire into a small tight loop to hold the stamen.
Thread the stamen stem through the loop.

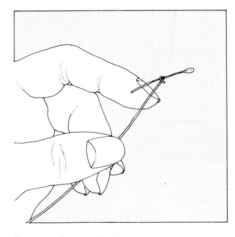

Repeat for each flower.

Step 3 To assemble the flower
Place the stem with stamen on the three-petal shape and dab a small amount of glue either side of the stamen. Squeeze the petals around the stamen to enclose it.

Take up the two-petal shape and lightly glue the base.
Complete the circle of petals by placing the base of the two-petal shape outside the three-petal shape. Cut a piece of No. 5 wire 7.5cm (3in.) long and wind it tightly around the base of the petals three times.

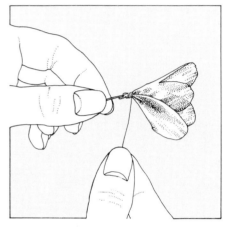

Twist the remaining end of the wire into the stem.
Wind floral tape around the base of the flower and down the stem.

Step 4 Finishing touches
Use your thumb and forefinger to open out the petals.
With a small pair of scissors curl the three-petal group inwards towards the stamen and curl the two-petal group outwards away from the stamen.

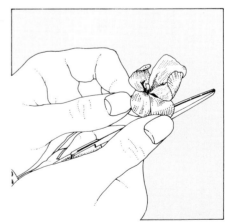

Bend the stem backwards from just below the base of the flower so that the two-petal shape is at the top of the flower.

Wild violet

The wild violet, recognized by its more trumpet-shaped head which nods over on the stem, is particularly suitable for waxing which gives it a delicate translucent quality. Pale yellow, pale blue or violet crêpe paper or a starched fabric like organza or a fine cotton will make very attractive flowers.

For a paper wild violet you will need:
The same materials as for the simple violet, except that the wild violet has an additional hooded sepal made from pale green crêpe paper (or thin fabric if making a fabric flower)

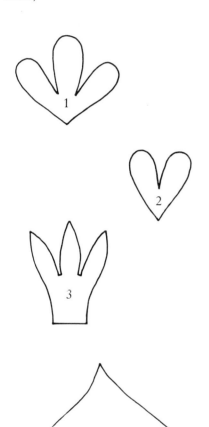

Step 1 To make the petals
Using patterns 1 and 2 cut out the petals in crêpe paper.
Assemble petals, stamens and stem as for the simple violet.

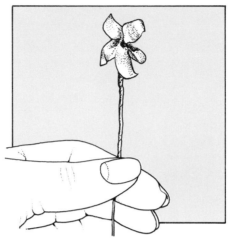

Bind the stem with floral tape and curl petals as for the simple violet.

Step 2 To make the sepals
Cut out sepal from pale green crêpe paper using pattern 3.
Place the center sepal behind the top two petals which are curled backwards.
Glue sepals around the base.
Bend the stem so that the head of the violet nods over.

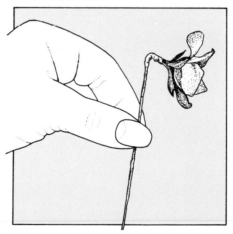

Step 3 To make the leaf
Using pattern 4 cut leaf shapes from folded dark green crêpe paper.
Cut pieces of No. 3 stem wire three times the length of each leaf and bind with floral tape.
Glue the covered wire between two leaf shapes to make one leaf.

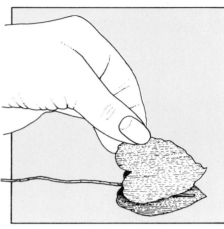

Score the leaf with the blunt edge of the scissor-blade to make veins.

Step 4 To wax the violets
Melt enough plain wax to cover the flower head when dipped (see page 17).
Dip the flower head only into the wax for a few seconds.
Shake gently to loosen any drips of wax.
Set aside to dry.

Left *A treasure chest of the smallest flowers — all made from fabric, and very decorative as a simple display in this old wooden box. From the left there are rows of purple simple violets made in cotton, velvet African violets, yellow polyanthus and multi-coloured forget-me-nots also in velvet. Next to these are the delicate organza rosebuds used in the hair in the picture on page 27, then pansies and velvet sweet peas. A small posy of each of the flowers sits in the drawer beneath the assembled rows of flower heads. More ideas for using these tiny flowers are displayed in the lid of the box. Greetings cards decorated with forget-me-nots and another with violets, dangling rosebud earrings as described on page 26, and the hair comb of violets as seen in the picture on page 69. A necklace with tiny wild violets and large forget-me-not flowers attached by their wires between the beads, gives a new lease of life to an old bead necklace.*

Right *Deep purple, yellow and pink violets in waxed paper are particularly unusual decorations for a dark chocolate cake. The larger waxed wild violets on this Valentine cake are flowers with their stems; the tiny simple violets with them are the flower heads only. Fine stamen stems are used to fix them to the chocolate before it sets.*

Left *Waxed violets have such a delicate glass-like quality that they can be used as you might use a treasured ornament, displayed either on a dressing table or shelf. Here a posy of violets was used with colored eggs as an Easter table decoration.*

Below *These wild violets of paper, in shades of palest blue to deep purple, have been lightly waxed. They provide a simple but charming greeting to the morning on a breakfast tray.*

HOLLYHOCK

This is how to make the whole hollyhock plant with buds at various stages of opening out and full flowers and leaves in different sizes. All these are mounted on a dowel stick or straight twig for support. You could plant it in a pot and stand it on the floor or use it with gladioli for a grand formal arrangement.

For a paper hollyhock you will need:
Crêpe paper for petals that has been dampened beforehand so that the edges are crinkled
Suggested colors: yellow, pink, cyclamen, dark red, orange
Green crêpe paper
No. 1 and No. 3 wire
Dowel stick or straight twig up to 90cm (3ft) in length
Quick-drying clear glue
Scissors
Wire cutters

Step 1 To make the flower
Make about eight single flowers in varying sizes but the same color for a complete hollyhock plant.
Cut from prepared crêpe paper long strips of varying widths from 10cm (4in.) for the largest flowers to 5cm (2in.) for the smallest.
Strips for the largest flowers can be up to 120cm (4ft) long and for small flowers 60cm (2ft) long.
Pleat and fold a strip of paper around and around to complete the rosette-like hollyhock flower. Make sure the most crinkled edge of the paper is uppermost.

Cut a 30cm (12in.) length of No. 3 wire.
Place the base of the flower in the middle of the wire, twist the wire around and let the two ends come together below the flower to form a stem.
Repeat for each strip of paper to make eight flowers.
Bind each flower base and stem with a strip of green crêpe paper.

Step 2 To make the buds
Make seven or eight closed buds to be placed at the top of the stem.
Cut squares of green crêpe paper from 5cm (2in.) to 7.5cm (3in.) square and stretch the paper slightly.
Make little balls out of scrap paper, slightly varying in size.
Put each one of these into the center of a square of green crêpe paper and wrap the paper around to form a bud, twisting the corners together at the bottom.
Cut a piece of No. 3 wire 15cm (6in.) long.
Place the base of the bud in the center of the wire, twist the wire around and bring the ends down to form the bud stem.
Bind tightly with a strip of green crêpe paper.

The larger buds are made in the same way as the flowers using strips of the same width, but shorter, to give the impression of half-opened flowers.
Make one or two in the same color as the main flower and bind the flower base, but do not cover the wire.
Cut the bud sepals from green crêpe paper using pattern 1.
Glue the sepals around the half-opened bud allowing 2.5cm (1in.) of the opening flower to show above the points of the sepals.
Now cover the stem with a green crêpe paper strip.

Step 3 To make leaves
Cut two leaf shapes for each leaf following pattern 2. These can be made in varying sizes.
Cut a piece of No. 3 wire, 5cm (2in.) longer than leaf, and bind with a strip of crêpe paper.
Dab glue down the center and around the edge of one leaf shape, put the wire down the center and place the second leaf shape on top. Press both together.
Score vein marks in the leaf with scissors or a knitting needle.

Step-by-step hollyhock

Step 4 To assemble the flowers, buds and leaves

Take either a dowel stick, a straight twig or very heavy wire for the main stem of the flower.

Place a small bud at the end of the stem and wrap its base with a long strip of green crêpe paper, 2.5cm (1in.) wide, to secure to the stem. Continue winding the paper down the stem, adding gradually larger buds as you do so on alternate sides of the stem. Lower down attach the half-open buds and eventually the flowers and leaves. (Arrange the

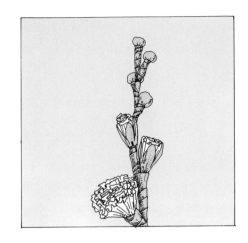

smaller flowers above the larger ones; the leaves should be below the flowers.)

The flowers should end about 20cm (8in.) from the base of the stem and more leaves can be grouped on longer stems coming out from the base.

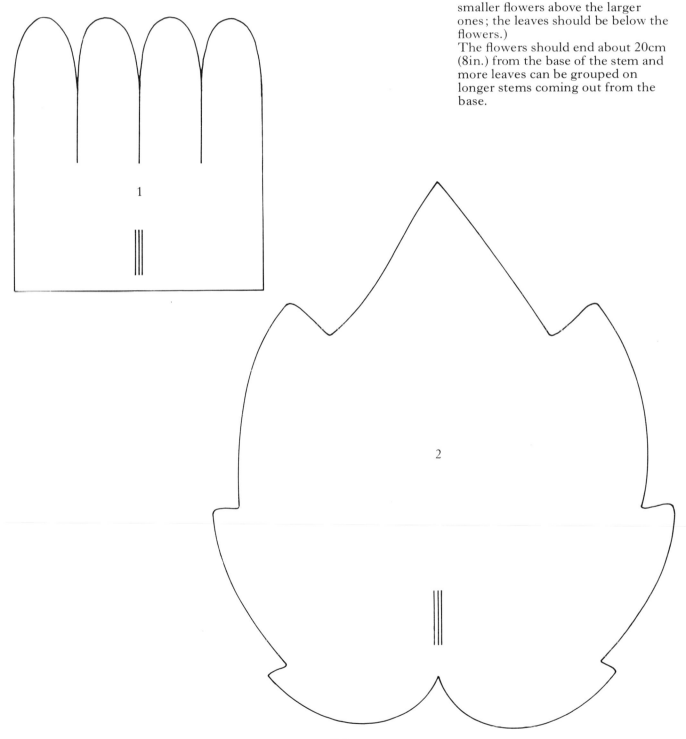

1

2

Above *Paper hollyhocks are fun flowers which require some patience to make if you want to make several whole plants, but are colorful and effective once you have made the effort. The individual flowers themselves are easy enough to make—so why not ask all the family to help? The tricky part is the assembling of the whole plant, leaves,* *flowers and buds onto the main stem, and this part shouldn't be left to junior! He can simply watch them grow. Hollyhocks are good plants to use to decorate a children's party; the bright colors and their simple shapes look particularly good against a plain brick or stone wall.*

Model garden

Left *A garden of indestructible flowers. This idea is specially for the children, who can have endless fun planning the flower beds and replanting their blooms. This is also an ideal way of using up reject flowers or those you have finished with. Cornflowers, daisies, pansies, violets, polyanthus, roses, primroses and forget-me-nots, made from paper and fabric, grow and flourish more quickly than the flowers from the often disappointing packet of children's seeds. This little boy played for hours re-arranging the rows and counting the flowers. After that he discovered that digging up the sand pathway and rolling it flat again was just as much fun.*

To make a model garden

The basic structure of the garden can be made from an unused tray, or for the base use an old shelf or other scrap wood. We made the base for our garden 50 × 100cm (20 × 40in.) and fixed 5cm (2in.) sides all around.

For the flower beds cut pieces of florist's foam about 1cm ($\frac{1}{2}$in.) thick and arrange as desired, but leaving space for pathways. Glue the florist's foam to the inside of the base. Sprinkle some soil over the top of the foam to give a thin covering. Put sand on the pathways and edge the flowerbeds with small stones.

Toy garden equipment makes the model garden even more fun. Flowers can be put in a miniature green house, the sand path rolled flat, and tiny dolls could be dotted around to make it look like a living garden.

If you wish to make a garden pond use a small mirror and surround it with moss or flowers to hide the edges.

PANSY

These pretty flowers look best when made in a smooth, soft velvet in yellow, blue or purple.

For a velvet pansy you will need:
Velvet that has been stiffened for petals
Suggested colors: yellow, mauve, burgundy, dark purple, blue or orange
Dark green velvet or satin that has been stiffened for leaves
No. 3 wire
Green floral tape
Quick-drying clear glue
Scissors
Wire cutters
Yellow poster paint
Black or dark blue felt-tip pen
Cotton wool (cotton)

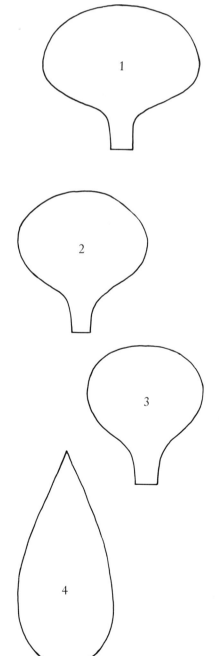

Step 1 To make the petals
Cut out one shape from pattern 1 in chosen color of velvet.
Cut out two identical petal shapes from pattern 2.
Cut out two identical petal shapes from pattern 3.
Using a felt-tip pen draw markings, from base and a little way up, on all petals except the two No. 3 ones.

Step 2 To make the stamen
Cut a 10cm (4in.) length of No. 3 wire.
Glue to one end a very small piece of cotton wool (cotton) and paint it bright yellow.

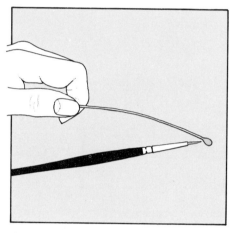

Cover the wire with floral tape.

Step 3 To assemble the flower
For each petal, cut a 10cm (4in.) length of No. 3 wire and glue down the center back.

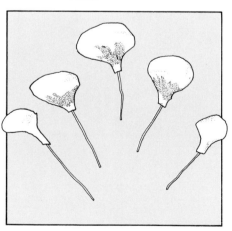

Glue the stamen head at the base of No. 1 petal.
Hold the two No. 2 petals on either side of this and twist petal and stamen stems together to form the main stem.

Bend the twisted stems backwards and up.
Turn the flower around so that these three petals become the lower petals.
Put a touch of glue on the base of the No. 3 petals.
Hold the flower facing you and attach the two No. 3 petals around the base of the stamen to become the upper petals.
Twist petal stems onto main stem.
Bind the stem with floral tape.

Step 4 To make the leaf

Using pattern 4, cut out the leaf in dark green fabric.
Glue a length of No. 3 wire, covered with floral tape and 5cm (2in.) longer than the leaf shape, down the center back.
Score vein marks on the leaf with scissors.
Twist leaf stem onto main stem.
Cover join with floral tape, if desired.

Step 5 Finishing touches

Bend flower head forward on its stem.
Bend the petals slightly forwards.
If you wish, cut a sepal shape in green cotton fabric from pattern 5 and glue it around the flower base.

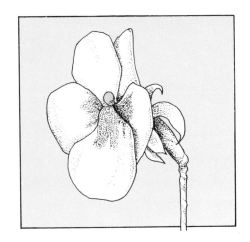

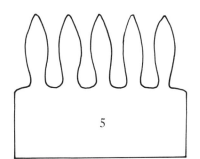

FORGET-ME-NOT

This is one of the simplest flowers to make and lends itself well to experimenting with different types of fabric, as well as crêpe paper.

For a fabric forget-me-not you will need:
Blue fabric for petals, either silk or cotton, which has been starched
Green fabric for leaves
No. 3 wire
Stamens from a hobby shop
Green floral tape
Quick-drying clear glue
Scissors
Wire cutters or pliers

Step 1 To make the flower

Using pattern 1 cut out flower shapes from the folded fabric.
Cut a length of No. 3 wire for each flower, 10cm (4in.) long.
Twist the end of the wire using wire cutters or pliers, making a small enough loop to hold the head of one stamen.
Place stamen head through the loop and bind the wire with floral tape.
Pierce a small hole in the center of the flower with the point of a scissor-blade and push the covered stem wire through.
Put a dab of glue at the base of the stamen so that it is fixed securely in the center of the flower.

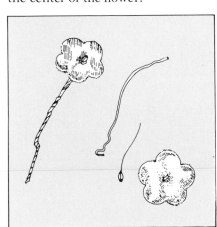

Step 2 To make the leaves

Cut several leaves in green fabric using pattern 2.
Cut several pieces of No. 3 wire each 2.5cm (1in.) longer than a leaf and cover with floral tape.
Glue the wires down the center back of the leaves.

Step 3 To assemble the flowers and leaves

Twist the stems of three or four flowers together starting at the bottom of the stems and working upwards for 5cm (2in.).
Add the leaves alternately down each side of the stem.

Step 4 Finishing touches

Bend the flower heads to face forwards and slightly away from each other.
Curve the leaves over and away from the stem.

Top *A collection of old bottles can look
even more decorative with flowers in them.
These are pansies made from velvet.*

Left *A velvet pansy brooch can be made
very easily. Simply attach the back of a
safety pin to the back of the pansy with a
dab of clear quick-drying glue as well as a
few light stitches to secure it.*

Above right *The large flat pansy makes an
unusual and effective bookmark. Here the
back of a velvet pansy is lightly stitched and
glued to a wide ribbon. The pansy flower
head without a stem can also be used.*

Ideas for forget-me-nots

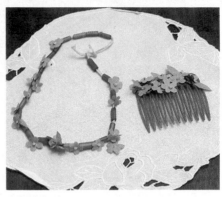

Left *This charming necklace and hair comb for a child is simple and quick to make. The forget-me-nots are made of cotton fabric. For the flowers for the hair comb, bind the short stems with floral tape. The flower heads and leaves are then glued directly onto the head of the comb.*

Above *The necklace is made from long glass beads which have been threaded onto fine white ribbon. The flowers each have a short length of No. 3 wire glued to the stamen head, behind the flower, and this is threaded through each bead. Each leaf is also glued to a short length of No. 3 wire and they are threaded through the beads in the same way.*

Above *The forget-me-not flowers look best grouped together to form a branching stem of flowers and leaves. These look particularly decorative on a hat.*

Right *This simple, pretty bunch of forget-me-nots made from velvet can be used to dress up a bag, skirt or hat. Once you have attached them, either by sewing or using a safety pin, you can then bend the stems to arrange the flowers as they look best. These forget-me-nots are much larger than the real flower and their unusual colors make a change from the delicate pale blue of the real flower.*

SWEET PEA

The sweet pea is an attractive flower, but complicated to make, particularly the fabric version. Once you have mastered it, experiment with different combinations of fabrics, such as velvet petals together with organza or silk ones.

For a fabric sweet pea you will need:
Velvet, silk, rayon or thin cotton fabric which has been stiffened for petals
Suggested colors: mauve, pale blue, pink, white
Green fabric for calyx and leaf
No. 1 and No. 3 wire
Knitting needle
Cup of boiling water
Floral tape
Quick-drying clear glue
Scissors
Wire cutters

For patterns, see page 83

Step 1 To make the petals
Cut one petal in chosen fabric from each pattern 1, 2 and 3.
The No. 1 petal can be of a darker shade fabric than the other two, or in a heavier fabric, such as velvet, while the other two are in silk or cotton.
Curl the two inner edges of No. 1 petal using a knitting needle, heated by standing it in hot water.
Curl No. 2 petal forward to face the front and No. 3 petal back.

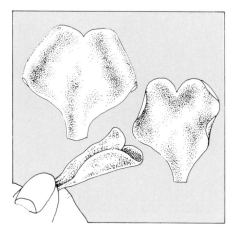

Step 2 To assemble the flower
Cut a 20cm (8in.) length of No. 1 wire for the stem and make a small hook at one end.
Put a dab of glue on the base of No. 1 petal and fold tightly around the stem enclosing the hooked end.
Pinch the fabric around the wire so that it will remain firm when dry.
Put a dab of glue on the base of No. 2 petal and fold around the first petal. It should curl forwards.
Put a dab of glue on the base of No. 3 petal and fold around behind the second petal, so that it curls outwards, away from the other petals.

Step 3 To make the calyx
Cut calyx in green fabric from pattern 4.
Dab glue on the calyx below the points and press around the base of the petals. (The overlap should be at the back of the flower.)

Step 4 To make the leaves and tendrils
Cut several leaves from green fabric using pattern 5.
Cut No. 3 wire for leaf stems, 2.5cm (1in.) longer than the leaves, and cover neatly with floral tape.
Glue the covered wire down the center of the leaves.
Make a tendril by covering a 15cm (6in.) length of No. 3 wire with floral tape and then twisting it around a knitting needle to shape it in a tight spiral, leaving 2.5cm (1in.) of untwisted wire.

Step 5 To assemble the flower, leaves and tendril
Twist a leaf stem to the straight end of the tendril wire and hold this next to the base of the flower with another leaf.
Bind over with floral tape to secure and continue winding all the way down the stem, adding other leaves if desired.

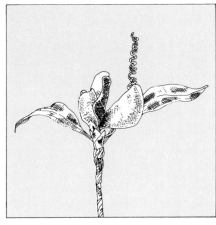

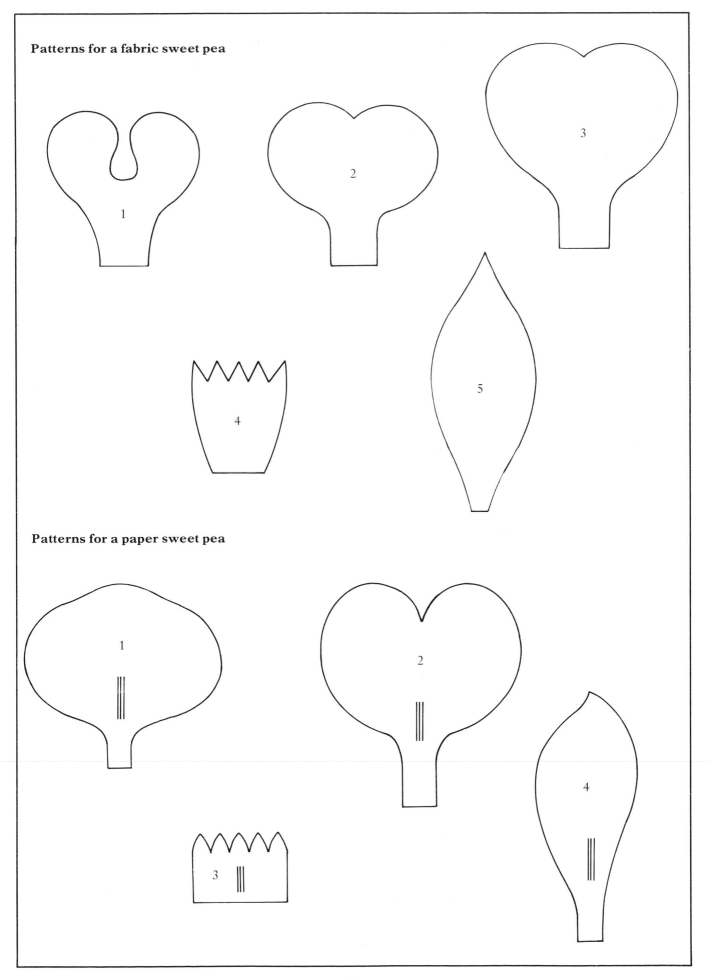

Patterns for a fabric sweet pea

1

2

3

4

5

Patterns for a paper sweet pea

1

2

3

4

Above *A bowl of organza sweet peas in palest pink, mauve, blue and deep pink have a much more delicate quality than those made from velvet. Their stems are covered with floral tape and they are placed in florist's foam to keep them standing upright in the center of the arrangement. Bend the heads and stems to face the way you want—this will make them look more natural.*

Left *Velvet sweet peas have a quite different character from other sweet peas, as this waistline posy shows. The heavier velvet with its own natural sheen gives them a richer and more glamorous quality. The stems are covered in the same pale green cotton fabric that is used for the calyx.*

Right *Sweet peas in paper are slightly more difficult to make than those in fabric, but once you have mastered the technique of folding the central petal, they look very pretty and fresh in their shades of pink and mauve. The tendrils are an unusual feature of the plant and fun to make—much easier than you'd expect. The sweet pea is a climber and you may wish to make trailing plants which can climb up an old trellis or wicker screen.*

85

For a paper sweet pea you will need:
Crêpe paper for petals in blue or pink
Green crêpe paper
No. 1 and No. 3 wire
Quick-drying clear glue
Scissors
Wire cutters

For patterns, see page 83

Step 1 To make the petals

Cut one petal shape from pattern 1 and cup lightly.
Cut one petal shape from pattern 2: flute the edges and cup the centre.
Curl the sides and top over a scissor-blade.

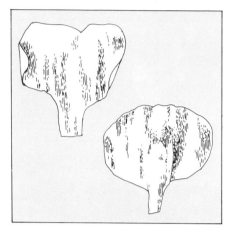

To make the central petal, cut a piece of crêpe paper 7.5cm (3in.) across the grain and 5cm (2in.) deep.
Fold the two corners of the 7.5cm (3in.) length into the center.
Fold back down the center line.

Gather together all four thicknesses in the middle of this petal shape, as indicated by arrows in the diagram.

Holding carefully with one hand, flute the open edges, stretching and pulling them down further so that all the free ends can be gathered together. If necessary bind lightly with No. 4 wire.

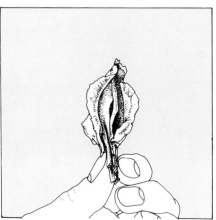

Step 2 To assemble the flower

Place the No. 2 petal around and behind the central petal with its curled edges facing forwards.
Place No. 1 petal behind this with its curl facing backwards away from the other petals.
Secure the bases of the petals with No. 3 wire, leaving a 7.5cm (3in.) length of wire for the flower stem.

Step 3 To make the calyx

Cut out the calyx shape in green crêpe paper using pattern 3.
Glue the calyx around the base of the petals, and stretch the points so that they curl over.

Step 4 To make the leaves and tendril

Cut six leaf shapes from pattern 4 in a double-thickness of green crêpe paper.
Cut No. 3 wire 2.5cm (1in.) longer than the leaves and cover with green crêpe paper.
Glue the wire down the center between two leaf shapes to make three leaves.
Take a 12.5cm (5in.) length of No. 3 wire and bind with green crêpe paper.
Wind around a knitting needle to make a curled tendril, leaving 2.5cm (1in.) uncurled.

Step 5 To assemble flower, leaves, tendril and stem

Cut a 25cm (10in.) length of No. 1 wire for stem.
Twist the straight end of the tendril to the end of the stem.
Hold the end of the stem with the tendril at the base of the flower and bind the flower stem to the main stem with No. 3 wire.
Attach the single leaves alternately down the main stem using their own stems to secure them.
Bind the joins and main stem with green crêpe paper.

APPLE BLOSSOM

These are instructions for making a large spray of blossoms and leaves mounted onto a real dry twig which gives a very natural effect. Choose an interestingly shaped twig with many short branches on which you can fix your blossoms. You will need 10 to 12 blossoms for a large spray.

For a paper apple blossom bough you will need:
White crêpe paper, preferably prepared to give it a pink edge, for petals and pale pink crêpe paper for bud
Yellow and light green crêpe paper
No. 3 wire
Quick-drying clear glue
Scissors
Wire cutters
A strong, dark wood twig

For patterns, see page 90

Step 1 To make the petals
Cut one strip of five petals from pattern 1 so that the pink coloring comes at tops of the petals. (If you have not prepared the paper, it is possible to paint the tips of the petals with pink once they have been cut out.)
One strip of petals makes one flower. Make as many flowers as desired.

Step 2 To make the stamens and sepals
These instructions are for making a lot of stamens.
Cut a long strip of yellow crêpe paper 2.5cm (1in.) wide.
Stretch and fold over four times.
Cut into 2.5cm (1in.) lengths.
Cut a fine fringe along one edge about 1cm (½in.) deep.
Twist the tips of this fringe into thin strands between your finger and thumb.
Cut one sepal shape from pattern 2 in pale green crêpe paper for each blossom and each bud.

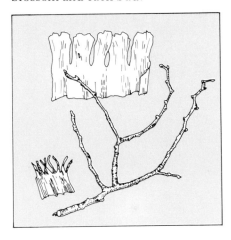

Step 3 To assemble the flower
Stretch each petal slightly across the broadest part.
Gather the strip of petals around the bunch of yellow stamens so that the tips of the petals are about 1cm (½in.) above the stamen ends.
Cut a 15cm (6in.) piece of No. 3 wire. Bind the flower at the base of the petals by placing it in the center of the wire and twisting the wire around; bring the ends down to form the flower stem.
Trim any surplus paper under the binding wire and neatly glue the sepals around the base of the flower. Open petals out.
Repeat for each blossom.

Step 4 To make the bud
Roll some scrap crêpe paper into a ball 2cm (¾in.) across.
Cover this with a square of pale pink crêpe paper, twisting the corners together underneath the ball.
Bind with No. 3 wire as for the flower and glue the sepals around the bud shape to cover the binding wire.

Step 5 To make the leaves
Using pattern 3 cut two shapes for each leaf in pale green crêpe paper.
Cut a piece of No. 3 wire 2.5cm (1in.) longer than the leaf.
Glue the uncovered wire between the two leaf shapes.
You will need six to eight leaves for this bough.

Step 6 To assemble the flowers, buds and leaves
Group flowers and buds together in clusters – three or four flowers and perhaps one bud at the top. Twist the stems together to secure.
Add one or two leaves just below the flowers.
Hold the twisted stem of the cluster to the twig and bind over with brown floral tape or a strip of brown crêpe paper to cover the join.
Add single leaves and blossoms on the smaller branches of the twig.

Above *Apple blossom casually placed on a sideboard, shelf or in a bowl of fruit as here, brings an unexpected touch of brightness to a corner of a room. The blossom is made of white crêpe paper tinged with pink around the edges.*

Left *The apple blossom has been wired and bound with crêpe paper to a real twig which has been cut short in this instance. The twigs are attached to the frame of the mirror with clear double-sided tape.*

Right *Apple blossom on long real twigs is very pretty and useful in a large arrangement of mixed flowers. The twigs are not as flexible as the wire stems so that arranging them involves the same care that you would have to take with real flowers, but the wooden stem does add an interesting and different texture.*

Above *Orange blossom, here made from white crêpe paper which has been waxed, is beautiful for a bride, and there will be no fear of it dying before the end of the day. The stems of the sprigs of blossom are wound around each other to make a garland. The stems can then be bound again with floral tape to cover the joins, if you wish. Twist the flowers into the position you want and secure the garland to the hair with hairpins.*

Right *Orange blossom for the bridesmaid, too—or even for a special party dress. Her friend was content with a pink ribbon round his neck !*
The individual sprigs of blossom are sewn firmly to the hem of the dress. This orange blossom is not waxed, and can be made from white crêpe paper or fine cotton fabric.

89

Patterns for apple blossom

1

2

3

Patterns for orange blossom

1

2

ORANGE BLOSSOM

These are particularly pretty when waxed. A spray of orange blossom consists of several flowers, buds and leaves and will require a lot of time to make. The result will be a delicate spray of flowers to wear in your hair or at your waist, or, if you make several, around the hem of your skirt for a party or carnival.

For a paper orange blossom spray you will need:
White crêpe paper for petals
Yellow and leaf green crêpe paper
No. 1 and No. 3 wire
Quick-drying clear glue
Scissors
Wire cutters

For patterns, see page 90

Step 1 To make the petals
Cut one five-petal shape from pattern 1 in white crêpe paper.
Cup petals near base and use scissors to curl each petal towards center.

Step 2 To make the stamens
Cut a strip of yellow crêpe paper 2.5cm (1in.) wide.
Stretch and cut into 2.5cm (1in.) lengths.
Cut a fine fringe 1cm ($\frac{1}{2}$in.) deep along one edge.
Gather into tight bunches.
This will make stamens for many blossoms.

Step 3 To assemble flowers
Gather a petal strip evenly around a stamen bunch with the stamen tips ending 1cm ($\frac{1}{2}$in.) below the petal tips.
Cut a 15cm (6in.) length of No. 3 wire.
Place the flower base in the middle of the wire, and twist the wire around to secure. Bring the two ends of wire down together to form the flower stem.
Cut off any surplus paper at the base of the flower.
Bind calyx and flower stem with a strip of green crêpe paper.
Bend petals back from flower center. Half-open flowers can be made by using three petals around the stamens and not bending them back.

Step 4 To make the bud
Gather a scrap of white crêpe paper into a ball about 1cm ($\frac{1}{2}$in.) across and pull into an elongated shape.
Cut a 5cm (2in.) square of white crêpe paper and cover the bud shape, twisting the ends together at the base.
Cut a 10cm (4in.) length of No. 3 wire.
Bind bud by placing the base in the center of the wire and twisting the wire around; bring down the two ends to form a stem.
Trim any surplus paper.
Wrap base of bud and stem wire with green crêpe paper strip.

Step 5 To make the leaves
Cut two shapes for each leaf from pattern 2.
Cut a piece of No. 3 wire 2.5cm (1in.) longer than leaf shape.
Glue the uncovered wire between the two leaf shapes.

Step 6 To assemble the flowers, buds and leaves
To make up a spray, the flowers, buds and leaves are attached to a piece of No. 1 wire. The length depends on the size of the spray.
Place the buds and half-open flowers at the top and the blossoms lower down with the leaves and twist the stems together.
Bind with a strip of green crêpe paper.

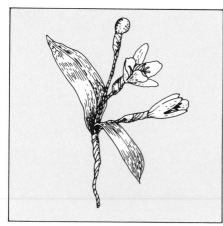

Ideas for stephanotis

These delicate and simple white stephanotis flowers are mixed with real leaves and dried flower heads. Some of the stems have been lengthened to give them more height. The leaves can be preserved by standing them in a mixture of hot water and glycerine first. This would ensure that your arrangement would last intact for a long while.

Inset *The stems of the stephanotis flowers have been wound around the plain white candlesticks to be used on the dining table instead of the more usual vase of flowers. If you wish to make them look more real, make the flower slightly smaller and pinch the petal tube together near its base. Real stephanotis have a waxy quality and the paper ones can be waxed to give this effect, as can the leaves.*

93

STEPHANOTIS

This flower lends itself well to waxing. It looks very decorative in an arrangement with fresh greenery, which offsets the white of the flowers. Stephanotis can also be made in stiffened white cotton fabric.

For a paper stephanotis you will need:
White crêpe paper for petals
Leaf green crêpe paper
Pale yellow poster paint or watercolor
No. 1 and No. 3 wire
Quick-drying clear glue
Scissors
Wire cutters

Step 1 To make the petals
Cut petal shape in white crêpe paper using pattern 1.
Stretch petals slightly across the broadest part.
Fold around into a cylinder shape and glue the two edges together.

Step 2 To make the stamens
Cut stamen shape from pattern 2 in white crêpe paper.
Along the shortest edge, cut fine strips 2.5cm (1in.) long to form a fringe.
Paint the tips of this fringe yellow. Allow to dry, then twist into thin strands between your finger and thumb.
Roll the strip around into a bunch of stamens.

Step 3 To assemble the flower
Slip the bunch of stamens into the center of the petal tube so that the stamens are 2cm (¾in.) below the petal tips.
Cut a 25cm (10in.) length of No. 3 wire.
Place the base of the flower in the center of the wire and bind it tightly around with three twists. Bring the ends of the wire down together to form the stem of the flower.

Stretch the petals out and back and squeeze the tube of the flower under the curl of the petals to make it narrower.

Step 4 To make the sepals
Cut a sepal shape in green crêpe paper from pattern 3.
Glue it around the base of the flower to cover the binding wire.
Take a thin strip of green crêpe paper and wind it around the stem. Stretch the points of the sepal away from the flower.

Step 5 To make the leaves
Using pattern 4, cut two shapes for each leaf in green crêpe paper.
Cut a length of No. 3 wire 7.5cm (3in.) longer than the leaf and bind with a green crêpe paper strip.
Glue the covered wire down the center of one leaf shape and glue the other leaf shape directly on top of it. Press firmly in place.
Score the main central vein and side veins with a knitting needle or scissors.

Step 5 To assemble flowers and leaves on main stem
Make five or six flowers and twist their stems together at base.
Cut a 25cm (10in.) length of No. 1 wire for the main stem and make a small hook at one end.
Put this hook into the twisted flower stems and bind with No. 3 wire, if necessary.
Cover the join and continue down the length of the main stem with a strip of green crêpe paper.
Leaves can be placed in pairs and arranged on the main stem. Bind them in place with No. 3 wire and cover joins with a strip of green crêpe paper.

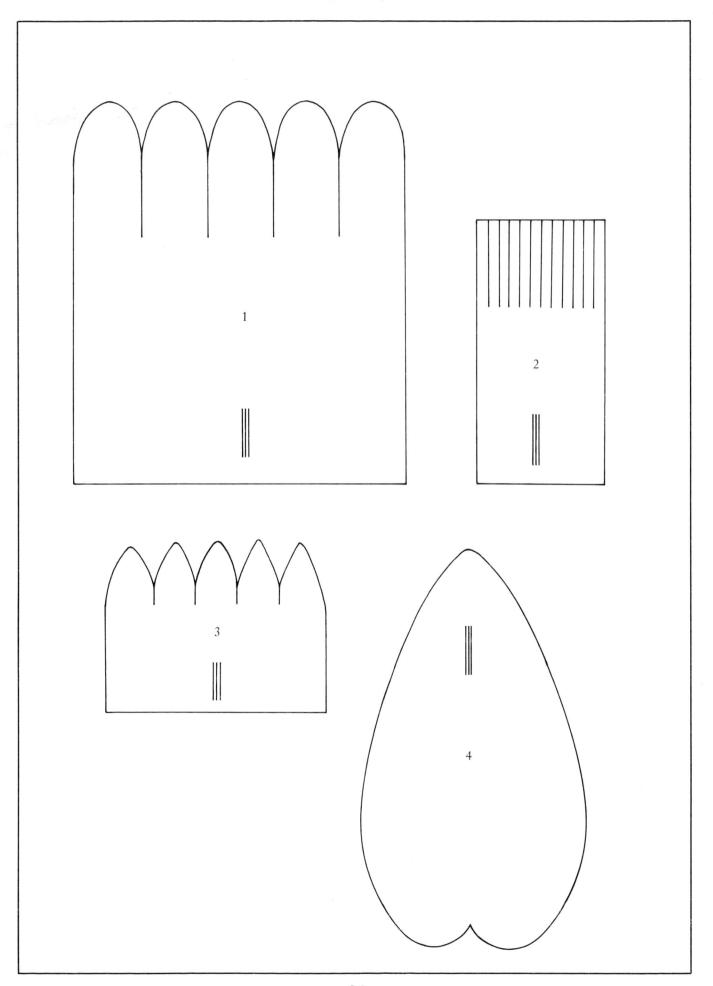

Above *Magnolia flowers and apple blossom look marvellous together in this large tree-like display—a splendid decoration for a special occasion, perhaps a conference or an exhibition or for the corner of a large room in your house. Any tall stand would be suitable, but it is important that it has a firm broad base as the flowers make it top heavy. The blooms are attached to real twigs which are stuck firmly into fine wire netting, which is packed tightly into the basket. The basket is itself tied with wire to the wooden stand.*

Left *Waxed magnolia flowers in a glass bowl make a pretty arrangement for a bathroom.*

MAGNOLIA

The magnolia flowers look best when fixed to a real twig. Keep some flowers more open than others for a very natural effect.

For a paper magnolia you will need:
Double-sided crêpe paper in shell pink for petals (a double-thickness of ordinary pale pink crêpe paper can be used as a substitute)
Yellow, green and brown crêpe paper (or brown floral tape)
No. 3 wire
Red pastel
Twig for main stem
Quick-drying clear glue
Scissors
Wire cutters

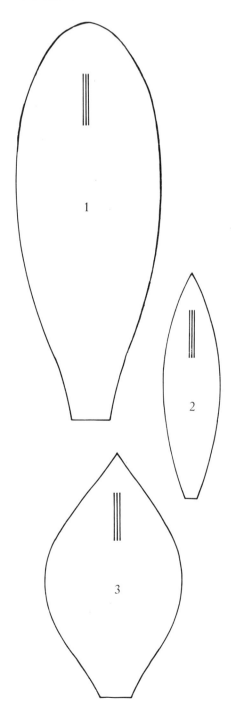

Step 1 To make the petals
Cut six petal shapes from pattern 1 in double-sided pink crêpe paper. Using a red pastel, color lightly from base of petals upwards, leaving the tips uncolored.
Cup petals with the red coloring on the outside.

Step 2 To make the stamens
Cut a piece of yellow crêpe paper 7.5cm (3in.) long and 3.5cm (1½in.) wide.
Cut a fringe 2cm (¾in.) deep along the long edge.
Twist the ends between your finger and thumb into strands for stamens.

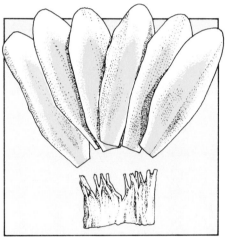

Step 3 To assemble the flower
Group three petals evenly around the stamens so that the red shading shows on the outside.
Keep the base of stamens even with the base of petals and bind with two twists of No. 3 wire to secure.
Put your fingers inside the base of petals and cup outwards.

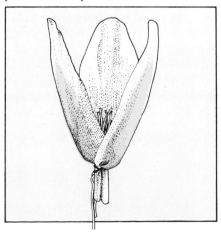

Place the three remaining petals in the spaces around the flower.
Bind by placing the flower in the center of a 15cm (6in.) length of No. 3 wire and twisting the wire around; pull the ends down together to form the flower stem.

Step 4 To make the sepals
Cut three separate sepals from pattern 2 in green crêpe paper.
Put a touch of glue on the base of each sepal.
Carefully glue one behind each outer petal.
Curl back from flower.

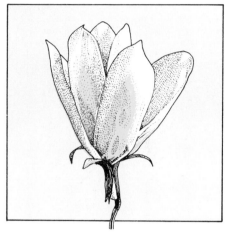

Step 5 To make the leaves
Cut two shapes for each leaf in a double-thickness of green crêpe paper using pattern 3.
Cut a piece of No. 3 wire 2.5cm (1in.) longer than the leaf.
Glue the uncovered wire between the leaf shapes.
Make three or four leaves.

Step 6 To assemble flowers and leaves onto main stem
Hold the flower in place on the end of the twig and bind the stem, starting from the flower base, with a strip of brown crêpe paper or floral tape.
Attach the leaves to the twig in the same manner—by holding the stem wires and twig together and binding them over.

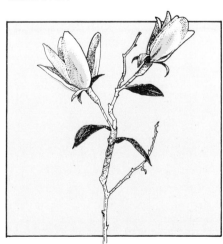

Above *The tall and spiky gladioli stems look best in a tall vase together with other flowers in a formal arrangement, or as here, lying in a basket as though freshly picked from the garden. Fresh flowers often look lovely when just picked lying in a basket in this way, but of course they can never be left like that as they need water. These paper gladioli can.*

Left *Baskets, of all shapes and sizes, are ideal for displaying paper and fabric flowers. Flower heads can even be used to disguise the worn edges of an old basket, and a selection of assorted flower heads look decorative in a shallow basket.*

Right *What a pity the paper gladioli don't thrive in the spring rain!*

GLADIOLI

Although the individual flowers are easy to make, it requires a good deal of time to make up the whole stalk with its flowers, buds and leaves. For an effective flower arrangement at least four large stems are needed—and, of course, the brighter the colors, the more striking the arrangement.

For a paper gladioli you will need:
Crêpe paper for petals
Suggested colors: yellow, orange, red, cyclamen or white
Green and white crêpe paper
No. 1 and No. 3 wire
Quick-drying clear glue
Scissors
Wire cutters
Straight twig or length of cane up to 60cm (24in.) long
Black felt-tip pen

Step 1 To make the petals
Cut four large petals from pattern 1 and two smaller petals from pattern 2 for each flower.
Glue three large petals together in a fan shape with one in the center and the other two behind on either side.

Now glue the remaining large petal in the center of two smaller ones in the same way.
Flute out the top edges of all the petals.

Step 2 To make the stamens
Cut a piece of white crêpe paper 5cm (2in.) square and cut a fringe 2.5cm (1in.) deep.
Stripe stamens with a black felt-tip pen to shade them.
Roll the fringe ends between finger and thumb to make separate strands.

Step 3 To assemble the flower
Gather stamens into a bunch and group the smaller three-petal shape around, but not completely enclosing, the stamens.
Place the larger group of petals facing these and wrap them around the stamens and the first group of petals.
Twist the middle of a 15cm (6in.) length of No. 3 wire around the base of the flowers, bringing the two ends down together to form the flower stem.

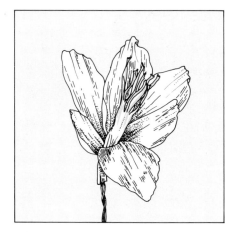

Step 4 Finishing touches for the flower
Cup the three large petals in towards the center of the flower. These are the upper petals.
Fold the other three petals outwards.
Make the large petal in the center of the lower group fold further down than the other two.
Make six or seven flowers for each stem.

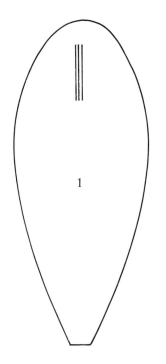

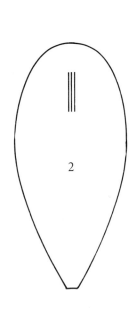

Step 5 To make the buds
Closed and half-open buds are usually seen growing on the same flower stem.
The closed, terminal bud is folded as for the madonna lily bud (see page 57) from a square of green crêpe paper 12.5cm (5in.) across.
Use 10cm (4in.) of No. 3 wire to secure the bud at the base and to form the stem.
Cover the binding wire and stem with a green crêpe paper strip.
The half-open, lateral buds are made from the same size square of crêpe paper but in the same color as the flower so that they resemble half-opened flowers.
Fold into bud shape as before. For the calyx cut two shapes in green crêpe paper using pattern 3 and fold around the colored bud.
Cut a piece of No. 3 wire 10cm (4in.) long.
Place the calyx in the center, twist around the wire to secure and bring down the ends to form the stem.

Step 5 To assemble the flowers and buds onto the main stem.
Hold the stem of the terminal bud alongside the straight twig or cane, so that the bud appears to be coming out of the top, and bind neatly together with a long strip of green crêpe paper.
Continue winding down the main stem, adding more green buds on alternate sides, then the half-opened buds, and lastly the flowers.
Place flowers alternately on either side of the stem and bend the heads forward to face the front.

Step 6 To make the leaves
Cut two shapes for each leaf in green crêpe paper using pattern 3. These should be 45cm (18in.) long and spear-shaped.
Cut a length of No. 3 wire 2.5cm (1in.) longer than a leaf and cover with green crêpe paper.
Glue down the center between the two leaf shapes.
Make two or three leaves for each flower stalk, and attach to the base of the stem, if desired.

Cover with a strip of green crêpe paper.
Make three to five of both kinds of bud for the complete flower stem.

3

This pattern is the actual size for the calyx. For the leaf make it 45cm (18in.) long.

Although irises mix very well with other flowers in a large arrangement these giant flowers are more dramatic alone in a striking art deco vase.

Inset A burst of fresh spring colors from these large paper irises, which could equally well be made in velvet or cotton.

IRIS

The iris is attractive in fabric as well as paper. Use velvet, silk or cotton fabric or a combination of two of them. Make dots of yellow poster paint for pollen grains.

For a paper iris you will need:
Crêpe paper in purple and blue for petals
Brown, yellow and green crêpe paper
No. 1 and No. 3 wire
Yellow pastel
One pipe cleaner
Quick-drying clear glue
Scissors
Wire cutters

Step 1 To make the petals
Cut a length of paper 65cm (26in.) wide and 12.5cm (5in.) deep and fold over six times lengthwise.
Lay pattern 1 diagonally across the grain of the paper.
Cut out to make six petal shapes.

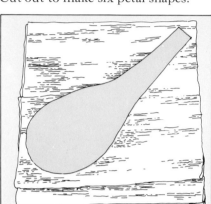

Cut six 15cm (6in.) lengths of No. 3 wire.
Glue wire in between pairs of petal shapes to make three petals.
Make three more petals from pattern 1 in lighter crêpe paper.
Cut out three shapes from pattern 2, also in the lighter crêpe paper, for stamens.
Cut out one shape from pattern 3 in brown crêpe paper.

Step 2 To make the pollen grains
Cut a narrow strip of yellow crêpe paper and make a very fine fringe. Cut off the fringe ends to make tiny pieces like confetti for pollen grains. Put a touch of glue in the center of the three darker petals and sprinkle on the pollen grains.

Step 3 To make the pistil
Use one pipe cleaner folded in half and twisted together.
Color yellow with pastel.

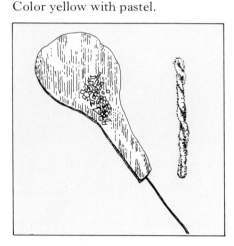

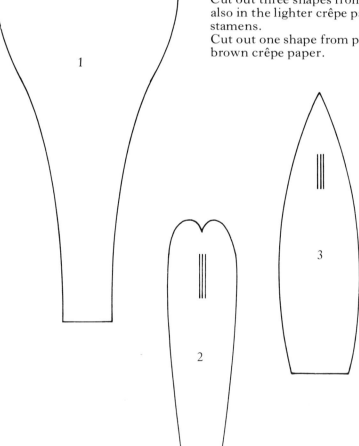

Step 4 To assemble the flower head

Curl each stamen shape around a scissor-blade.

Group the three stamen shapes around the pistil with the curls facing inwards.

Arrange the three dark petals, dotted with pollen grains, evenly around the stamens.

Place the three lighter petals alternately between them.

Bind the bases of all petals together with No. 3 wire.

Step 5 To make the leaves

Cut out four leaf shapes from pattern 4 from a double-thickness of crêpe paper.

Cut two lengths of No. 3 wire, 2.5cm (1in.) longer than the leaf shapes, and bind with green crêpe paper strip.

Glue the covered wire between the leaf shapes to form two leaves.

Step 6 To attach the flower, stem, sheath and leaves

Cut a 45cm (18in.) length of No. 1 wire.

Make a small hook 1cm ($\frac{1}{2}$in.) from the end.

Push the wire down the center of the petals so that the hook is embedded in the base of the flower.

Bind the flower base once more with No. 3 wire.

Bind the stem with green crêpe paper strip, incorporating the brown sheath 3.5cm (1$\frac{1}{2}$in.) below the flower. The leaves can be incorporated opposite each other lower down the stem.

Step 7 Finishing touches

Bend the three dark petals dusted with pollen out and then down.

Bend the three lighter petals out and then up, curving towards the center.

Flute the top edges of the six petals very lightly.

Bend the flower head over by bending the stem between the flower head and the sheath.

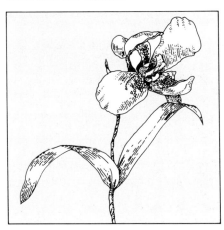

4

Left *A large basket of paper narcissi in a bathroom or bedroom is a simple decoration but it can look very attractive.*

Right *A touch of spring indoors while there is still some snow outside. These narcissi will brighten up the house even when the end of the winter is still far away. The crêpe paper has a fresh, crisp quality particularly suitable for these simple flowers.*

Below *These paper flowers look surprisingly natural next to the fresh salad ingredients. Here's one good way of filling an empty strawberry pot with its array of holes from top to bottom.*

NARCISSUS

Both the narcissus and daffodil look best made out of paper as it gives a fresher, crisper look. It also lends itself better to waxing, if desired.

For a paper narcissus you will need:
White crêpe paper for petals
Green, yellow and brown crêpe paper
No. 1 and No. 3 wire
Red ink
Quick-drying clear glue
Scissors
Wire cutters
Drinking straws

Step 1 To make the petals
Cut six petal shapes in white crêpe paper using pattern 1.
Cup across the broadest part.

Step 2 To make the flower center and stamens
Cut a strip of yellow crêpe paper from pattern 2.
Roll around your finger or pencil and glue down the side to make a tube shape.
Flute out the top.

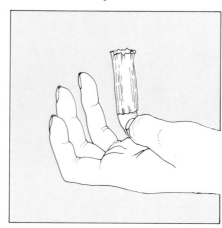

To make three stamens, cut a strip of yellow crêpe paper 1cm (½in.) across the grain and 3.5cm (1½in.) deep.
Make two cuts, equally spaced, 2.5cm (1in.) deep down the grain.
Roll each strand between your finger and thumb to make three separate stamens.
Slip these into the center of the yellow paper tube, gather at base and bind with two twists of No. 3 wire.
Touch fluted edge with a brush dipped in red ink.

Step 3 To assemble the flower
Arrange three petals around the base of the yellow flower center. (Put a touch of glue on the petal bases, if desired.)
Add the three remaining petals in the spaces around the flower, and bind with three twists of No. 3 wire.

Open out the petals to lie almost flat. Cut a piece of No. 1 wire the length of the drinking straw for the stem and make a small hook at one end. Push the wire down through the flower to one side of the trumpet so that the hook remains embedded in the calyx.

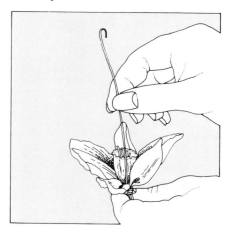

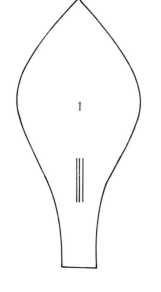

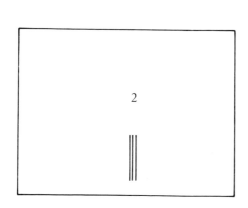

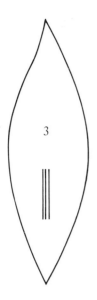

3

Step 4 To strengthen stem and attach sheath
First cut sheath in brown crêpe paper using pattern 3.
Place the flower stem inside a drinking straw. The stem can now be trimmed, if desired.

Press the straw flat up one side.
Wind a strip of green crêpe paper down the stem, starting at the flower base and covering the binding wire.
Attach the sheath about 3.5cm (1½in.) down the stem.
Continue binding the stem to cover it completely.
Bend the flower head forward away from the sheath.

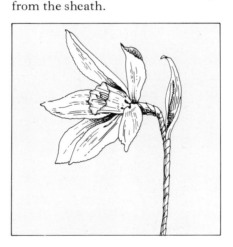

Step 5 To make the leaf
Leaves are optional for use in arrangements.
Cut two shapes for each leaf in green crêpe paper, using pattern 4.
Cut a piece of No. 3 wire the same length as the leaf and glue between the two leaf shapes.

Daffodil

The daffodil is made in the same way as the narcissus except that all the petals and the flower center are yellow. The daffodil flower center is about 1cm (½in.) longer and a small amount wider than that of the narcissus, and the edge of the flower center should not be painted with red ink.

4

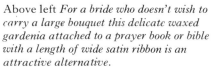

Above left *For a bride who doesn't wish to carry a large bouquet this delicate waxed gardenia attached to a prayer book or bible with a length of wide satin ribbon is an attractive alternative.*

Above right *Paper and waxed gardenias with glass tulips in a simple modern vase, make an unusual ornament.*

Left *and right This pure white gardenia, which has been waxed, makes an elegant accompaniment to a glamorous evening.*

GARDENIA

This flower is not easy to make, but is a very delicate and elegant decoration for a hat or a dress. It can also be made in a fine velvet. The paper gardenia looks particularly good when waxed.

For a paper gardenia you will need:
White crêpe paper for petals
Green crêpe paper
No. 1 and No. 3 wire
Quick-drying clear glue
Scissors
Wire cutters

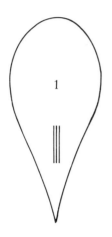

Step 1 To make the petals
Cut 17 petal shapes from pattern 1. These are shaped in four different ways:
First, flute the top of three of the petals (No. 1) and cup each one.
Secondly, curl eight petals over a scissor-blade (No. 2) and cup each petal, holding it with the curl towards you.
Thirdly, curl the sides of two of the petals with the scissor-blade (No. 3) and cup each petal, this time holding it with the curl away from you.
Fourthly, simply cup the remaining four petals (No. 4).

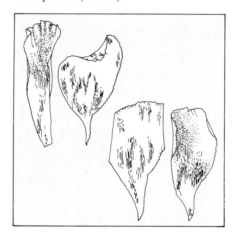

Step 2 To assemble the flower
You can glue the petals as you add them to the flower, if necessary.
Take one No. 4 petal and roll into a cocoon shape, placing two No. 4 petals around it.
Add a No. 1 fluted petal followed by the last No. 4 plain petal.
Put the eight No. 2 curled petals around the flower.
The two fluted No. 1 petals are added last, curling away and down from the rest of the flower. They should fall away from the center of the flower.

Cut a 20cm (8in.) length of No. 3 wire.
Place the flower base in the center of the wire, twist the wire around and bring down the two ends.
Bind this with green crêpe paper.

Step 3 To make the bud
Cut three more petal shapes from pattern 1 for the bud.
Flute one of these, curl the remaining two lightly over the scissor-blade.
Cup all three bud petals.
Assemble together with the fluted petal in the middle, the two curled petals surrounding it and bind the base as for the flower with a 15cm (6in.) length of No. 3 wire, bringing the ends of the wire together to form the bud stem.
Bind the bud stem with green crêpe paper.

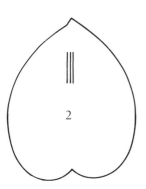

Step 4 To make the leaves

Cut out four leaf shapes, using pattern 2, from a double-thickness of green crêpe paper.
Cut pieces of No. 3 wire slightly longer than the leaf and glue, uncovered, down the center of each pair of leaves.

Step 5 To assemble the flower, bud and leaves

Using a long narrow strip of green crêpe paper, bind the flower stem again, incorporating the first leaf blade flush with the stem 2.5cm (1in.) below the flower. (More leaves can be added, if desired.) Incorporate the second leaf in the same way onto the bud stem.
To join the bud stem to the flower stem simply hold the stems together and bind over with green crêpe paper.

If a longer stem for a vase arrangement is required, add a piece of No. 1 wire cut to desired length along the side of the flower stem and bind together with green crêpe paper.

Potted Plants

Although flowers made from paper and fabric have always been popular, it is unusual to come across a potted paper aspidistra! These plants are very easy to make and provide a lot of fun. They make marvellous gifts—and, of course, you don't need to talk to them to keep them alive!

Potting your plants

Potted plants, both the flowering and the leafy variety, are enjoyable to make and fun to have around the house. They also make original and very welcome presents.

The plants can be made of crêpe paper or of fabric. Try waxing the leaves too. Some of these then look really lifelike for many indoor plants have leaves with a waxy sheen. Do remember that if you are using fabric which will be bleached to make the leaf markings, it is best to use a white or cream fabric and dye it green yourself. Fabric already factory-dyed may produce strange and unexpected colors when bleached. It may work, but test a small piece first to be sure that you are going to achieve the effect you want. You may be able to create some interesting effects this way!

Flower pots, baskets, bowls
The advantage of paper and fabric indoor plants is that they don't need soil or water, so you have a much wider choice of vessels in which to

For example, a tall jardinière with a glossy-leaved aspidistra or palm in it can look very elegant.

Whether you use clay flower pots or plastic ones, the fact that the pot has or does not have holes in the bottom is now irrelevant. If you use plastic pots, why not try painting them bright colors to match or contrast with the plants. Be inventive with the pots you choose, as well as your flowers. Window boxes, troughs of wood or clay, or even china, are suitable for these indoor plants and can transform the look of a window without a view.

Stabilizers
Although your paper and fabric plants don't need soil or water they do need something to stabilize them in their pots. Many of them are made up from a number of single separate leaves which are assembled together in the pot to make the whole plant. Florist's foam or styrofoam pushed down securely into the pot will adequately hold the plants.

ways of doing this. If you live in the country and can find moss growing naturally it will make an excellent disguise. Even when it has dried out it will still look good. Soil, lightly sprinkled on the top of the florist's foam, or even filling the pot completely, is also very effective. If you don't want to give the appearance of reality simply cover the foam with green or brown crêpe paper, or thin fabric, before you insert the wire stems.

Large top-heavy plants, such as the palm, really do need a tall narrow-necked pot or to be placed in a

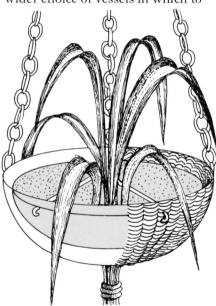

Secure florist's foam in a hanging basket by pushing two lengths of wire over the top of the foam, and hooking the ends through the basket.

Leaves fixed in florist's foam covered with a layer of moss.

A top-heavy plant should be placed in a bottle and the bottle wedged with wood or styrofoam in a large plant pot.

plant them. Even open-work baskets and wire baskets are suitable. All you need to remember is that if you are using florist's foam to help support the plant this should not show through the sides of the container. Unusual china pots can also be used to make a very distinctive display and you should not be afraid to give your plants the same sort of grand treatment you would give a real palm or aspidistra.

Alternatively, fine-mesh wire netting, shaped to form a mass and fit tightly inside the pot, can also be used. For a plant with a delicate leaf stem or, for example, the daffodil with its paper straw and wire stem, it is best to make a hole first in the florist's foam with a pencil in order not to damage the stems when they are pushed in.

If you want to disguise the florist's foam in a small pot there are various

heavy, narrow-necked bottle wedged inside another pot. Anything heavy that you can attach to the plant's base with wire will also do the trick.

Many paper and fabric plants, particularly those like the ivy or other trailers which don't have to be 'rooted', don't need a pot at all. If you like the idea of a trailing ivy around your balcony or alcove it can seem to appear from nowhere!

AFRICAN VIOLET

Use different shades of purple and pink velvet or organza prepared with size or starch for the flowers and dark green velvet for the leaves. This plant is made up of about 12 flowers and 12 leaves so it is a good idea to fold the fabric and cut out as many as possible at the same time.

For a fabric African violet you will need:

Purple or pink starched velvet or organza for petals
Dark green velvet for leaves
Double-headed stamens from a hobby shop
No. 3 wire
Green floral tape
Quick-drying clear glue
Wire cutters or pliers
White chalk
Pencil
Small scissors

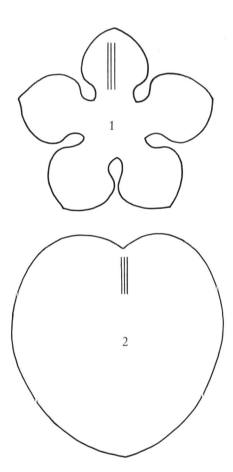

Step 1 To make the flowers

Using pattern 1 cut out 12 petal shapes.
Make a small hole in the center of a petal shape using the point of a scissor-blade.
Cut a 11cm (4½in.) piece of No. 3 wire and twist the end of the wire into a small loop.
Taking two double-headed stamens, bend each in half and put them together to create a four-headed stamen.
Thread them through the stem wire loop and twist the stamen stems around the wire to secure them.

Push the wire through the hole in the center of the petals.
Put glue on the wire beneath the stamens, pinch the petals together towards the stamen center and arrange the petals.

Wrap the stem with floral tape.
Make 12 flowers.

Step 2 To make the leaves

Using pattern 2 cut out several leaf shapes in dark green velvet.
To make veins, take a pencil and score the velvet.

Lightly mark the areas between the score marks with white chalk and dust off with your fingers to give a soft natural look.
Cut a length of No. 3 wire three times the length of the leaf and bind with floral tape.
Glue the covered stem wire down the center back of the leaf, stopping just short of the tip.

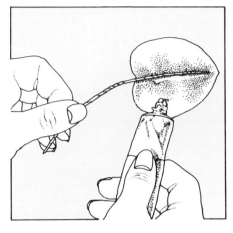

Bend the leaf downwards very slightly to give a more natural appearance.
Make 12 leaves in this way.

Step 3 To make up the potted plant

Divide the single flowers into groups of four and twist their stems together halfway up from the base to make three flower heads.
Fill the plant pot with florist's foam.
Put the stems of both leaves and flowers into the foam, arranging the flowers in the center and the leaves around the edge.
Cover the foam with moss or so desired, although the leaves and flowers should hide it if they are carefully arranged.

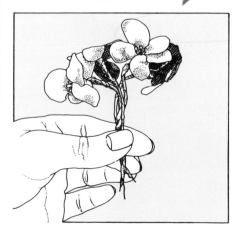

Above *Pots of African violets on a window ledge can give a feeling of spring in the air the year round. These African violets are made from velvet in a variety of colors, and the flowers are arranged, with the leaves around them, in florist's foam packed tightly inside the pots. Real flower pots, or colored ceramic pots as shown here, are more stable and attractive than plastic pots.*

Right *This potted African violet has organza petals, which give it a more delicate appearance and contrast well with the velvet leaves.*

Above *The paper aspidistra is a very versatile plant and fun to have around the home—or office. It will look good both in a modern room and in the kind of setting in which it flourished in its heyday during the Victorian and Edwardian eras.*

Left *The aspidistra leaves are made individually and put into florist's foam which is packed tightly into a suitable plant pot or basket. The leaves can then be arranged the way you want. This plant can be quickly transformed from a tall and upright one to one of very different character yet equally unmistakable as an aspidistra.*

ASPIDISTRA

This pot plant is fun and easy to make. Just make sure you have a large amount of paper before you start. The leaves can be arranged as desired to make it either a tall upright plant or a flatter one with the leaves arranged to fall over the sides of the flower pot. It looks its best when made of paper with the leaves highly varnished.

For a paper aspidistra you will need:
Leaf green crêpe paper
No. 1 wire
Quick-drying clear glue
Scissors
Wire cutters
Varnish
Potting materials

Step 1 To make the leaves
Leave the roll of crêpe paper folded and draw a simple leaf shape on one side, of length 50cm (20in.) and 12.5cm (5in.) at the widest part.

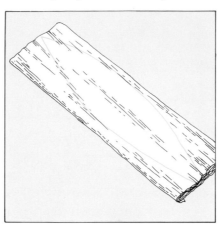

Cut through the folded crêpe paper to make several identical leaf shapes. Put the shapes together in pairs and trim some pairs to make a variety of leaf sizes.
Cut No. 1 wire lengths 10cm (4in.) longer than the leaves.
Cover wire with a strip of green crêpe paper.
Take one leaf shape from each pair and put glue down the central vein and all around the edge.
Place the covered wire down the center of the leaf, put the other leaf shape on top and press together firmly.

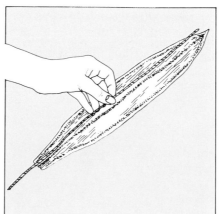

Spray each finished leaf liberally with varnish.

Step 2 To assemble the plant
The edges of the smaller leaves should be curled around a pencil and placed in florist's foam in the center of the flower pot so that they appear to be new leaves just opening.
Stretch the larger leaves across the widest point to broaden them and place around the younger leaves. Curl leaves over and out from the center and arrange so that some appear to be growing higher than others.

PALM

This is a very impressive decorative plant, but it is complicated to assemble and needs an experienced hand for best results.

For a paper palm you will need:
Leaf green and brown crêpe paper
No. 1 and No. 3 wire
Quick-drying clear glue
Scissors
Wire cutters
Potting materials

Step 1 To make single leaves

Leave the crêpe paper folded and draw long spear-like leaf shapes on one side.
These should be 35cm (14in.) long and 3.5cm (1½in.) at the widest point.
Cut through the thicknesses of crêpe paper to make several identical leaf shapes.
Put the leaf shapes together in pairs and trim some pairs so that the final number of leaves is as follows:
Seven leaves 15cm (6in.) long. (These will be the terminal leaves.)
Fourteen leaves 17.5cm (7in.) long; fourteen leaves 20cm (8in.) long; fourteen leaves 22.5cm (9in.) long; fourteen leaves 25cm (10in.) long; twelve leaves 27.5cm (11in.) long; six leaves 30cm (12in.) long; six leaves 32.5cm (13in.) long and two leaves 35cm (14in.) long. (These will all be lateral leaves.)
The number of single leaves detailed above will give you seven main palm leaves or fronds.
Cut lengths of No. 3 wire for each leaf stem, 2.5cm (1in.) longer than the leaf.
Glue the uncovered wire between the leaf shapes.
Trim, if necessary, to neaten the edges of the leaves.

Step 2 To assemble the terminal and lateral leaves

For seven palm fronds first cut seven 60cm (2ft) lengths of No. 1 wire.
Cut a very long strip of green crêpe paper 2cm (¾in.) wide from the top of the roll of crêpe paper.
Twist the stem of one terminal leaf to the top of one main stem wire and bind over with green crêpe paper to cover the join.

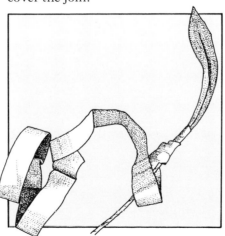

Twist stems of two 17.5cm (7in.) lateral leaves onto the main stem exactly opposite each other 2cm (¾in.) down from the terminal leaf. Wind the crêpe paper strip around the main stem and cover the joins of these leaves.
Continue adding pairs of leaves in this way, the leaves gradually becoming longer so that you finish with the two 35cm (14in.) leaves. Leave no more than 2.5cm (1in.) gaps between the pairs of leaves. Make sure that the joins at the main stem wire and the leaf stems are neatly covered as the crêpe paper strip is wound down to cover the stem.

Now you have a finished palm frond.
Make two more palm fronds of this size.
Make three smaller palm fronds using only five pairs of lateral leaves and one frond using only four lateral leaves.
Bend all the leaves so that they are lying flat, but curling slightly backwards.

Step 3 To assemble the plant

Trim main stems of palm fronds to desired lengths. The smaller palm fronds have shorter stems and are arranged in the center of the plant. Hold all stems together and bind 15cm (6in.) of the way up with brown crêpe paper strip.
If necessary, add dowel for support. As the palm is a top heavy plant it may need to be supported by placing in a bottle or narrow jar before being put in a heavy plant pot.
If you want a very tall palm add dowel up to 120cm (4ft) long to each frond and put all of these into a large heavy stoneware jar.

Above *Spot the paper palm! Paper plants are shown mixing happily together in this restaurant with real plants. The one to look twice at is the large palm on the right of the archway.*

Right *The palm is one of the more difficult potted plants because of the way the leaves are assembled onto the main stem. However, the end result is worth all the trouble.*

Above *Ivy plants are mixed with geraniums in this window box.*

These ivy plants look different when placed side by side in a window box, though they are made from the same pattern. This is achieved by using different materials, as well as showing two ways in which they can be grown.

The paper ivy on the left is made from green crêpe paper which has been bleached to give a pattern to the leaves. The stem with leaves along it is then attached to a strong stick with wire, the base of which is fixed in florist's foam in a plant pot or window box.

The fabric ivy on the right is made from stiffened cotton fabric which was dyed a soft green color before stiffening. The creamy-white markings are made by bleaching.

The ivy stems are covered with floral tape and can be bent to shape the plant into a trailing plant, or can be tied to a stick to appear to grow upright.

Left *Potted plants are very suitable to brighten up a bathroom. Just be careful not to splash them or they might wilt!*

IVY

This plant can be made to do all sorts of things—climb tall on a support or trail down. It can also be made in crêpe paper using a double-thickness of paper for the leaves.

For a fabric ivy plant you will need:
Sage green (home-dyed) cotton fabric that has been starched
No. 1 and No. 3 wire
Green floral tape
Quick-drying clear glue
Scissors
Wire cutters
Bleach
Paint brush
Potting materials

Step 1 To make the leaves
Cut as many leaves out of fabric as required using patterns 1, 2 and 3.
Cut lengths of No. 3 wire for each leaf. These can vary from 7.5cm (3in.) for small leaves to 12.5cm (5in.) for larger leaves.
Cover lengths of wire neatly in green floral tape.
Glue the wire down the back of the leaves and allow to dry.
Paint bleach around the edges of the leaves to give a variegated effect and allow to dry.

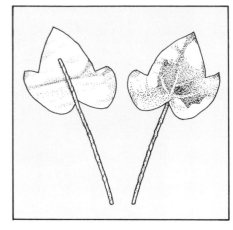

Cut main stem to desired length from No. 1 wire and cover in floral tape.
Twist stem wires of leaves together in clusters with the bigger leaves in the center and the smaller leaves growing outwards in trailers.
Twist onto main stem.
Arrange leaves to lie flat so that most of the stems are covered.
For potting, put the main stem in florist's foam in a flower pot.

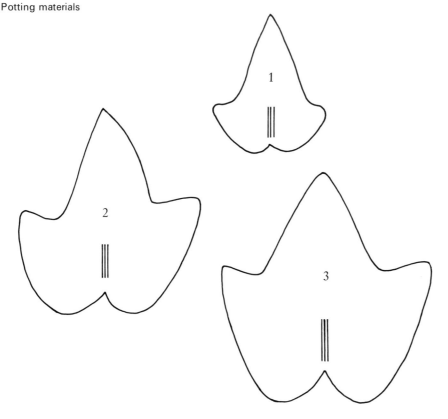

SPIDER PLANT

This plant can be very attractive when made up in stiffened fabric. The leaves are cut from only one thickness of the fabric, and the stems are made from wire covered with floral tape and glued to the back of each leaf. Remember that when marking leaves with bleach, you should use home-dyed fabrics for best effect.

For a paper spider plant you will need:
Leaf green crêpe paper
No. 1 and No. 3 wire
Quick-drying clear glue
Scissors
Wire cutters
Bleach
Fine paint brush
Potting materials

Step 1 To make the large leaves
Leave the crêpe paper folded and draw a long spear-like leaf shape on one side.
This should be 40cm (16in.) long and 3.5cm (1½in.) at the widest point. (It is possible to fit two leaf shapes of this size on one side of folded crêpe paper.)
Cut through the thicknesses of crêpe paper to make several identical leaf shapes.
Put the leaf shapes together in pairs and trim some pairs to make a variety of leaf sizes.
Cut No. 1 wire lengths 10cm (4in.) longer than the leaves and cover each with a strip of green crêpe paper.
Take one leaf shape from each pair and put dabs of glue down the central vein and all around the edge.
Place the covered wire down the center of the leaf, placing the other leaf shape on top and pressing firmly together.

Step-by-step spider plant

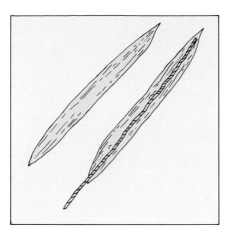

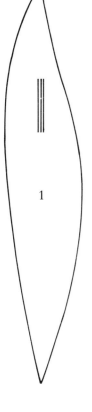

1

You will need approximately 20 leaves of varying sizes for a full plant.

Step 2 To make leaves for the plantlet
Cut smaller leaf shapes from pattern 1.
Cut in pairs as for the long leaves and trim to make a variety of sizes. You will need six to eight leaves of the same size for each plantlet, and one or two plantlets per plant.
Cut a piece of No. 3 wire 2.5cm (1in.) longer than the leaves.
Glue the uncovered wire between the leaf shapes.

Step 3 To mark the leaves
Mark the large leaves and plantlet leaves in the same way, by painting a stripe of bleach neatly down the center of each leaf. Make the stripe very thin as the bleach tends to be absorbed outwards and spread.

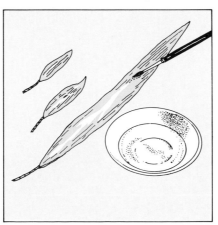

Wait for bleach to dry and the markings to appear.

Step 4 To assemble the plantlets
Cut a length of No. 1 wire from 30cm (1ft) to 60cm (2ft) long and attach six to eight plantlet leaves to one end by twisting the wires together.
Bind the join with a strip of green crêpe paper to cover all the wires and continue binding down the complete length of the plantlet stem.
Bend leaves over so that they hang down.

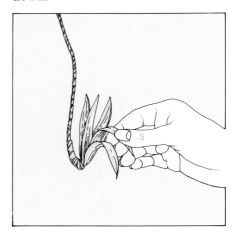

Brush bleach along the stem of the plantlet so that it turns white.

Step 5 To assemble the plant in a plant pot
Put the large leaves into florist's foam in a large pot and bend them over so that they hang down the side of the pot.
Arrange the plantlets so that they trail down at the front of the plant pot.

Ideas for spider plants

Right *and below Spider plants are fun, particularly when they have several small plantlets growing from them. They are ideal for placing in hanging baskets. The leaf stems are fixed into florist's foam which is wired to the basket for stability.*

Ideas for hostas and hydrangeas

Left *The large broad leaves of the hosta plant can be made in either paper, as seen here, or in fabric. It is a bold, dramatic plant and would go particularly well in an office in need of a little greenery to relieve its starkness.*

Below *The flower heads for this potted hydrangea plant took several hours to make —but it was worth it! This plant is one of the more difficult to make as the florets, though quite simple, are small and not so easy to handle as the larger flowers. The leaves give a tremendous boost to the finished plant, as their dark green color is a perfect foil for the delicate pink flowers.*

HOSTA

This plant can be made equally well in paper or fabric. Use white cotton fabric dyed green—an ideal way of reusing old sheets and pillow-cases.

For a paper hosta plant you will need:
Green crêpe paper
No. 1 wire
Quick-drying clear glue
Scissors
Wire cutters
Bleach
Fine paint brush

Step 1 To make the leaves
Cut about six to eight leaves of varying sizes for a full plant. Make a template following the shape given in pattern 1. For a larger leaf draw a line on cardboard 1cm ($\frac{1}{2}$in.) all around the first leaf pattern and cut out. Repeat, using this second template as the basis for an even larger leaf. Cut two shapes for each leaf, making sure the grain of the paper runs from top to bottom of the leaf.

Cut lengths of No. 1 wire, 10cm (4in.) longer than the leaves, and bind with a green crêpe paper strip. Glue wire between leaf shapes.

Step 2 To mark the leaves
Draw veins onto the leaf with a pencil. Paint bleach onto each leaf very carefully, following the vein marks. As bleach spreads, make the lines very fine. Wait for bleach to dry.

Step 3 To assemble plant
Put leaves into florist's foam in a flower pot. Bend over and away from center.

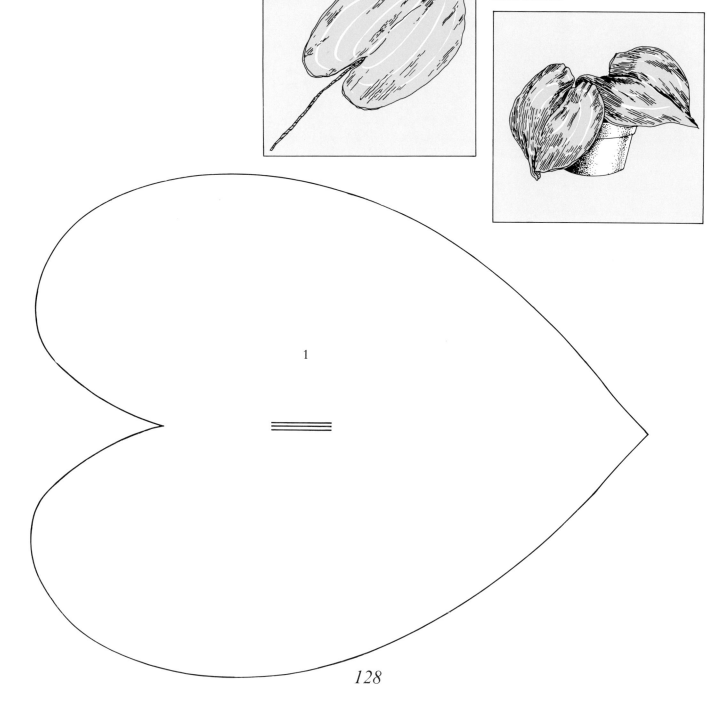

1

HYDRANGEA

This flower can also be made in a fine cotton fabric. It requires patience to make as each flower consists of about 24 small individual florets.

For a paper hydrangea you will need:
Crêpe paper in pink, blue or mauve for the petals
Green crêpe paper
No. 1 and No. 3 wire
Scissors
Quick-drying clear glue
Wire cutters
Pliers
Stamens from a hobby shop

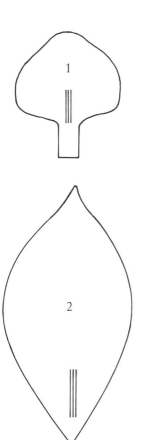

Step 1 To make a single floret
Take a piece of crêpe paper 15cm (6in.) long by 3.5cm (1½in.) deep and fold in half and then in half again to make four thicknesses. Using pattern 1 cut out four petals at the same time, which will be sufficient for one floret.
Stretch each petal very slightly across its width.

Step 2 To make the stem with a stamen
Cut a 10cm (4in.) length of No. 3 wire and twist the end into a tiny loop with pliers.
Thread a stamen through the loop and twist the stamen stem around the wire.

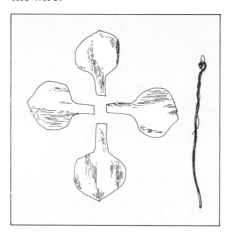

Step 3 To assemble the single florets
Put a touch of glue on each petal base and attach in pairs opposite each other around the stamen wire.
Holding the floret at its base, flatten out the petals.

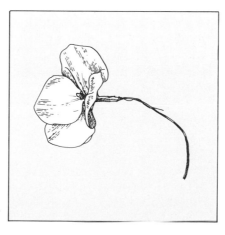

Cover the stem with green crêpe paper.
Repeat for 24 florets.

Step 4 To assemble the florets to form the hydrangea head
Divide into groups of four florets each and bind the bases of their stems together, 2.5cm (1in.) below the florets, using green crêpe paper. Twist these stems together.
Cut a 25cm (10in.) length of No. 1 wire, make a hook at the end and hook it in among the twisted stems. Cover with green crêpe paper and wind down the stem.

Step 5 To make the leaves
Cut out leaf shapes using pattern 2 from a double-thickness of crêpe paper.
For each leaf cut a piece of No. 3 wire, 3.5cm (1½in.) longer than the leaf, and bind with green crêpe paper.
Glue the wire between the leaf shapes.
Make about six leaves for each flower and attach to the main stem in pairs.
The edges of the leaves can be trimmed with pinking shears, if desired.

Ideas for polyanthus

Left *A potted plant as a gift is always welcome, but when it is made from velvet it is more of a surprise. This potted polyanthus, with flowers in soft shades of pink, would be an unusual gift at any time— and a lasting one.*

Right *Beautiful begonias—a china pot with a plant bursting with color will brighten up any corner.*

Below *Polyanthus plants are easy to make and very effective—try them out in colors which are wildly different from the natural flowers. The flowers can also be made singly and put together in a vase on their own or arranged with other small flowers.*

POLYANTHUS

This is a satisfying flower to make because, despite the fact that we specify the material, you can use any fabric you like and you will have good results.

For a fabric polyanthus you will need:
Velvet or brushed denim for petals
Suggested colors: yellow, deep purple, deep pink, mauve, pale blue
Soft green velvet or brushed denim for the leaves
Stamens from a hobby shop
No. 3 wire
Quick-drying clear glue
Scissors
Wire cutters
Deep yellow poster paint and a fine brush
Potting materials

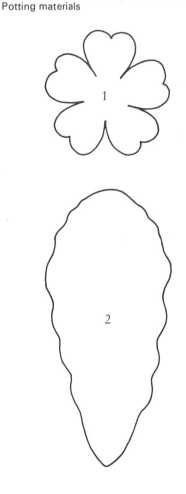

Step 1 To make the flower heads
Cut a flower shape in chosen color from pattern 1.
Cut a 15cm (6in.) length of No. 3 wire and make a very small hook at the end of the wire by twisting it tightly with the blunt edge of wire cutters.
Place a single stamen head in the hook.
Cover the wire with floral tape.
Put a dab of glue underneath the stamen at the top of the stem and push the wire through the flower center so that the stamen sticks to the center of the flower.

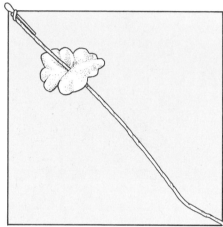

Paint a star-like shape around the stamen in the center of the flower with yellow poster paint.

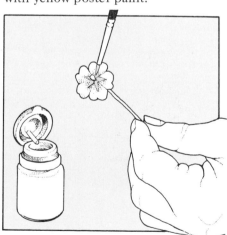

Make six or eight flowers for each polyanthus potted plant.

Step 2 To make the leaves
Cut a leaf shape in soft green fabric using pattern 2.
Cut a length of No. 3 wire 3.5cm (1½in.) longer than the leaf.
Trim the leaf shape around the edge to give a crinkled effect.
Cover wire with floral tape, and glue down the center back of the leaf.
Score vein marks in fabric with scissors.
Make 12 leaves.

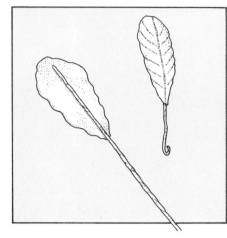

Step 3 To assemble the plant
Twist the stems of the flowers together 5cm (2in.) below the flower heads.
Splay out so that all the flower heads are visible from the top.

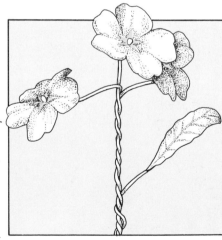

Put the stems into florist's foam in the flower pot and arrange the leaves around the flowers, bending them back towards the rim of the flower pot.

BEGONIA

This flower is prettiest when made with tinted paper. White paper with a hint of pink looks very delicate.

For a paper begonia you will need:
Prepared crêpe paper for petals
Suggested colors: shades of pink and white
Green crêpe paper
No. 1 and No. 3 wire
Scissors
Quick-drying clear glue
Wire cutters
Varnish
Potting materials

Step 1 To make the flowers
Cut a strip of prepared crêpe paper 7.5cm (3in.) wide and 75cm (30in.) long with the grain of the paper running vertically.
Fold over seven times and, using pattern 1, cut the three-petal shape out of the folded crêpe paper.
Unfold the petal strip and cup each petal shape.
Curl the top of the petal over a scissor-blade towards the cup.
Starting at one end, begin to roll up the petal strip, fairly tightly to begin with, and gradually becoming looser.

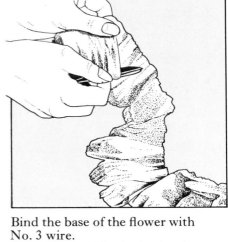

Bind the base of the flower with No. 3 wire.
Cut a piece of No. 1 wire for the flower stem at least 20cm (8in.) long.
Make a small hook at one end and push the wire down through the center of the flower base.
Cover base of flower and stem with a strip of green crêpe paper.
Open petals out to flatten the flower head.

Step 2 To make the leaves
Make as many leaves as desired for either a single bloom or a small potted plant.
For one leaf, cut two leaf shapes in green crêpe paper using pattern 2.
Cut No. 3 wire 5cm (2in.) longer than the leaves.
Cover the wire with a green crêpe paper strip.
Glue wire between the leaf shapes.
Fold so that there is a dip down the centre of the leaf and bend over and away from the stem.

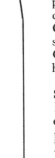

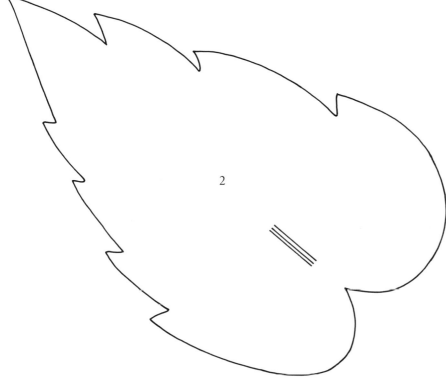

Step 3 To assemble the pot plant
Fill the flower pot with florist's foam.
Take three or four flowers and twist the stems together at the base.
Twist enough leaves around the flower stems to make a bushy plant.

Top *and* above right *For pots of crocuses such as these take care to cut the florist's foam to fit perfectly into the shape of the bowl you are using ; cover the top of it with soil if you wish. The flowers and leaves are made from cotton fabric that has been stiffened and they are a fresh reminder of spring.*

Left *Crocuses and tulips mix well together and these, made of paper, provide a vivid contrast with the terracotta flower trough in which they stand.*

Right *Tulips made from paper in shades of yellow and orange provide a focal point while blending beautifully with the colors in this cool and restful room without a view.*

134

CROCUS

The crocus can be made in both paper and fabric; use taffeta, silk or a fine cotton. The paper can also be tinted; a combination of pale and deep purple is particularly effective. The fleshiness of the petals can be achieved by cutting the petals from a double-thickness of paper although our instructions are given for a single-thickness. And the paper crocus can be waxed too.

For a paper crocus you will need:
Crêpe paper in chosen color for petals
Suggested colors: purple, orange, yellow, white
Leaf green and orange crêpe paper
No. 3 wire
Quick-drying clear glue
Scissors
Wire cutters

Step 1 To make the petals
Cut two three-petal shapes from pattern 1 in chosen color of crêpe paper.
Stretch paper across the base of the petals so that the tips of the petals curl inwards.

Step 2 To make the stamens
Cut a strip of orange crêpe paper 5cm (2in.) deep.
Stretch and fold over lengthways several times.
Cut a fine fringe 2.5cm (1in.) deep.
Open out the fringed strip and cut off 3.5cm (1½in.).
Roll fringe ends between your finger and thumb to make separate strands for stamens.
Gather stamens into a bunch.

Step 3 To assemble the flower
Wrap first one and then the other three-petal shape around the stamens.

Place the base of the petals in the center of a 25cm (10in.) length of No. 3 wire and secure by twisting around the wire. Then bend the two ends of the wire down together to form the flower stem.
Cover flower base and stem with green crêpe paper strip.

Step 4 To make the leaves
Cut two shapes for each leaf in green crêpe paper using pattern 2.
Cut a length of No. 3 wire, 2.5cm (1in.) longer than leaf, and glue, uncovered, between leaf shapes.
Make two leaves for each flower.

Step 5 Finishing touches
Put your fingers inside the flower and press outwards at base of petals to stretch the paper slightly.
Attach the leaves to the base of the flower stem by twisting the stems together and covering join with crêpe paper strip.

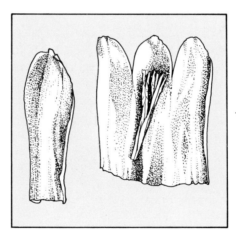

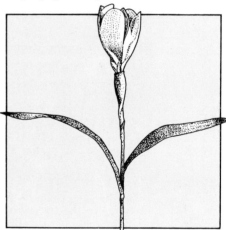

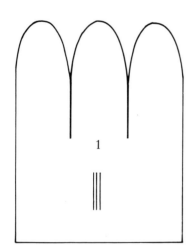

TULIP

The tulip is a flower which may be waxed to give it a natural sheen. It can be very effective in a double-thickness of paper, where you cut two identical shapes for each petal and glue them together.

For a paper tulip you will need:
Crêpe paper in chosen color for petals
Suggested colors: bright red, orange, yellow or pink
Light green, leaf green and black crêpe paper
No. 1 and No. 3 wire
Quick-drying clear glue
Scissors
Wire cutters
Paper drinking straw

Step 1 To make the flower center and stamens
Cut a 5cm (2in.) square from light green crêpe paper.
Fold the square in half and roll it lengthways into a short cylinder.
Hold together with a touch of glue.
Cut a black stamen strip 5cm (2in.) deep and cut a fine fringe 2.5cm (1in.) down.
Roll fringe ends between your finger and thumb to make separate strands for stamens.
Cut off a strip of six stamens to wrap around the light green center, and glue in place.

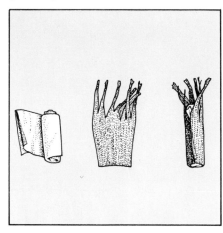

Put the rest of the fringe aside to be used for other flowers.

Step 2 To make the petals
Cut six petals from pattern 1 in chosen colour of crêpe paper.
Cup each petal.

Step 3 To assemble the flower
Put a dab of glue on the base of each petal and arrange three petals evenly around the stamen and center.
Place the remaining three petals in the gaps.
Bind the base of the flower with No. 3 wire.
Trim off surplus paper and wire for a neat finish.

Cut a piece of No. 1 wire as long as the drinking straw and make a small hook at one end.
Push this down into the flower to one side of the center.
For the stem place wire inside a paper drinking straw and press the straw flat up one side.
Cover flower base neatly with green crêpe paper strip and continue winding all the way down the stem.

Step 4 To make the leaf
Cut two shapes for each leaf in green crêpe paper using pattern 2.
Make a leaf 15–17.5cm (6–7in.) long.
Cut a length of No. 3 wire 2.5cm (1in.) longer than leaf shape.
Cover wire with a green crêpe paper strip and glue down center between leaf shapes.
Attach to the main stem by twisting the two stems together, starting at the base of the main stem and ending halfway up.

Step 5 Finishing touches
Arrange the petals by placing your fingers inside the flower and stretching the paper outwards just above the binding wire.
Curl leaf over backwards.

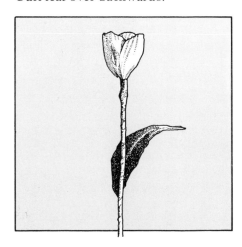

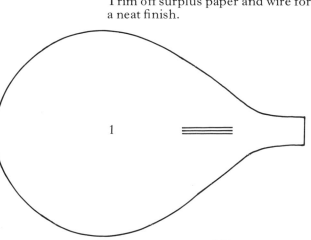

A hanging basket of geraniums and ivy made from paper—an exceptionally attractive display which doesn't need watering, the drawback to a hanging basket of real flowers. Take care to arrange the flower and leaf stems equally all the way around the florist's foam in the basket or you will find that the weight of the flowers will pull it over. Alternatively, secure the florist's foam to the basket with wire.

Inset This large terracotta pot has been made for planting strawberries, different kinds of herbs or flowering plants in its openings. Its natural color sets off the brilliant red of the geraniums. It is a useful display pot for paper and fabric flowers of all kinds, as they have the advantage of needing neither soil nor water. Trailing ivy mixed with a variety of flowering plants to add color also looks particularly good in this kind of pot.

GERANIUM

Geraniums are simpler to make than they might appear. And they're very adaptable: put a single flower in a small pot or several flowers together will look very attractive in a hanging basket. Make them in shades of deepest red to palest pink.

For a paper geranium you will need:
Crêpe paper for petals in red or pink
Green crêpe paper
No. 1 and No. 3 wire
Quick-drying clear glue
Scissors
Wire cutters or pliers
Brown pastel
Potting materials

Step 1 To make a floret

To make one flower head you will need up to 20 florets so it is advisable to cut as many flower shapes together as possible.
Cut petal shapes from pattern 1.
Cut a 15cm (6in.) length of No. 3 wire and make a very small hook at the top of the wire.
Take two petal shapes, putting one on top of the other, and push the wire through so that the hook is resting in the center of the petals.
Put a touch of glue around the hook and pinch the petals together from underneath so that they bunch up together to form a floret.
Bind the stem tightly from the base of the petals with a narrow strip of green crêpe paper.

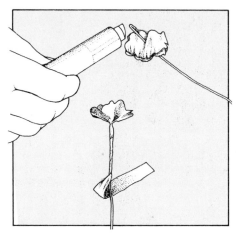

Step 2 To make the bud

Cut a 3.5cm (1½in.) square of crêpe paper in the same color as the florets and fold into a bud shape as for the madonna lily (see page 57).
Place the base of the bud in the center of the wire, twist the wire round, and bring the two ends down together to form the bud stem.
Bind the stem with a narrow strip of green crêpe paper.

Step 3 To assemble the flower head

Gather together 10 to 15 buds and 10 to 15 florets and twist the bases of the stems around each other with the florets and buds splaying out to form an umbrella shape.

Step 4 To make the leaves

Cut two shapes for each leaf in green crêpe paper using patterns 2 and 3.
Cut the crêpe paper with the grain running across the leaf shape. You can also vary the size of the leaves even more for a natural look.
Cut No. 3 wire stems for each leaf 5cm (2in.) longer than leaf shape.
Cover with green crêpe paper strip and glue between pairs of leaf shapes. Score with scissors or knitting needle to make veins.
Make a band 2.5cm (1in.) wide in the center of the leaf with brown pastel, following the outline of the leaf.

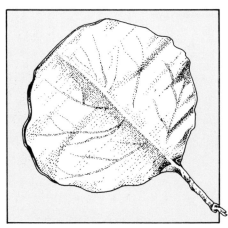

Make two or three leaves for each flower head.

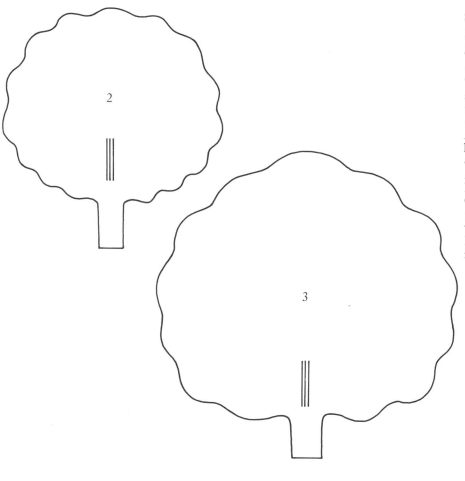

Step 5 To assemble the plant for potting

Use No. 1 wire for the main stem. The length depends on the size of the plant.

Twist the stems of one flower head and two or three small leaves together at the base and twist them onto the main stem.

Add other flower heads and small leaves lower down the stem, if desired.

Add the larger leaves to the lower half of the plant.

Cover the main stem with a strip of green crêpe paper so that all the wire and joins are covered.

Place the geraniums in florist's foam in a flower pot.

Special Occasions

Whether the occasion is a party or carnival, a ceremony, a family celebration, part of the festive season or an event which calls for large formal flower arrangements, the following ideas will certainly put into practice all you have learnt so far. Don't be afraid to be ambitious with your flowers—they look their best when there are lots of them together.

CHRISTMAS FLOWERS

Christmas is a marvellous opportunity for making paper, fabric and waxed flowers which are quite different, perhaps, from those you have made before or during the rest of the year.

This is really the time for using shiny paper and glitter, for making fun flowers with fanciful centers, as well as for taking advantage of the natural greenery available as a base for your displays.

The details of how to make the Christmas flowers shown on the following pages are given below and the instructions for constructing the arrangements and other Christmas ideas follow on pages 146–7 and 149.

Poinsettia

This is not an easy flower to make but it is very striking when finished. For a Christmas arrangement it can be made in gold and silver foil.

For a paper poinsettia you will need:
Bright red crêpe paper for the bracts
Yellow and leaf green crêpe paper
No. 1 and No. 3 wire
Quick-drying clear glue
Scissors
Wire cutters

Step 1 To make the bracts
Cut all the bracts in a double-thickness of red crêpe paper so that you have two identical shapes for each bract.
Cut three small bracts from pattern 1, four medium-size bracts from pattern 2 and five large bracts from pattern 3, using templates.
Cut 12 lengths of No. 3 wire, each 5cm (2in.) longer than a bract.
Glue the wire lengths between the bract shapes so that each bract has a stem of uncovered wire.

Step 2 To make stamens
Cut a strip of yellow crêpe paper 1cm (½in.) deep and 45cm (18in.) long. Make a fringe halfway down. Cut six equal lengths off the fringed strip.
Take one length, put glue along its uncut edge and fold tightly around a 10cm (4in.) length of No. 3 wire.

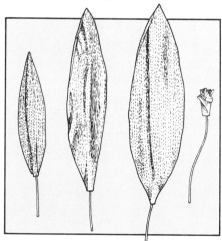

Repeat for the other five yellow strips to make six stamen heads.

Step 3 To assemble the flower
Twist the wires of the stamens together into a bunch.
Then place the three smallest bracts evenly around the stamens and twist their stems together. (The stamens should just cover the base of the bracts so that no stem wires can be seen from the top of the flower.)
Repeat for the medium-sized bracts.
Finally place the larger bracts in the remaining gaps.
Cut a 30cm (12in.) length of No. 1 wire for the stem and make a small hook at one end.
Place the hook in among the twisted stem wires at the base of the bracts.

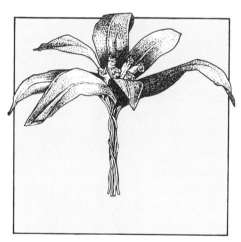

Cover the twisted wires neatly with a strip of green crêpe paper, binding all the way down the stem.

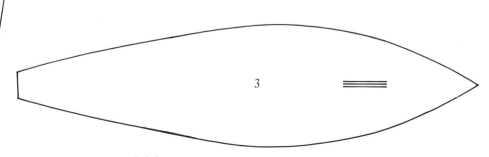

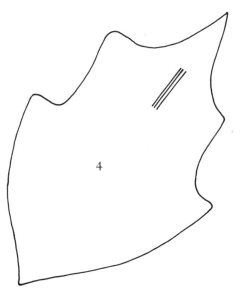

Step 4 To make the leaves

For each leaf, cut two leaf shapes in green crêpe paper using pattern 4. Cut a piece of No. 3 wire, 2.5cm (1in.) longer than leaf, and glue, uncovered, between the leaf shapes. Score vein marks with scissors. Make two leaves for each flower stem. Twist the leaf stem onto the flower stem and cover the join with strip of green crêpe paper. Add leaves alternately down the stem.

Christmas rose

This is ideal for waxing, whether made of paper or fabric. When making it from fabric use a thin white cotton. Each individual petal can be waxed before assembling the whole flower.

For a paper Christmas rose you will need:
White crêpe paper for petals
Green crêpe paper
No. 1 and No. 3 wire
Sisal twine
Pale green pastel
Yellow poster paint
Quick-drying clear glue
Scissors
Wire cutters

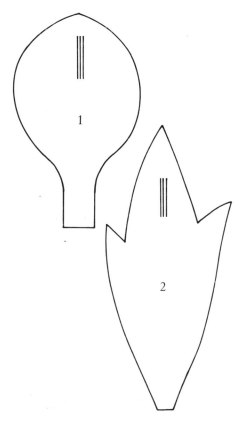

Step 1 To make the petals

Cut ten petal shapes from pattern 1 in white crêpe paper. Glue the petal shapes together in pairs to make five petals.
Color from the base to the middle of each petal with pale yellowy-green pastel, smudging it to give a smooth, matt finish.

Step 2 To make the stamens

Cut 5cm (2in.) of sisal twine and splay out into separate strands at one end.

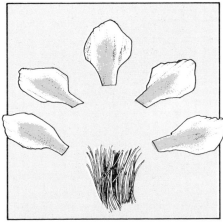

Dip this end into yellow poster paint and allow to dry.

Step 3 To assemble the flower

Arrange the five petals evenly around the stamens which should come halfway up the petals.
Bind at the base by placing the flower in the middle of a 25cm (10in.) piece of No. 3 wire and twisting the wire around; bring the ends of the wire together to form the flower stem.
Stretch and open the petals away from the flower center.

Bind stem with green crêpe paper strip.

Step 4 To make the leaf

Cut two leaf shapes for each leaf in green crêpe paper using pattern 2. Cut a piece of No. 3 wire, 5cm (2in.) longer than the leaf, and cover with a strip of green crêpe paper. Glue the covered wire between the leaf shapes. Attach the leaf to the flower stem about halfway up.

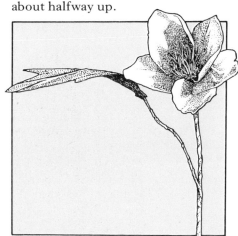

145

This festive scene shows poinsettias, Christmas roses, a mixed arrangement of paper and fabric flowers, together with brightly colored plastic fruits and real flower heads which have been dried. A garland of paper flowers with fresh greenery and ribbon provides a welcome at the door.

Metallic rose

Here is a fun flower for Christmas to make up in multi-colored metallic paper.

You will need:
Metallic paper in chosen color
Crêpe paper for stem
Dried poppy seed head on stalk (or substitute with a tight roll of crêpe paper glued to the top of a strong piece of stem wire)
No. 3 wire
Glitter
Quick-drying clear glue
Scissors
Wire cutters

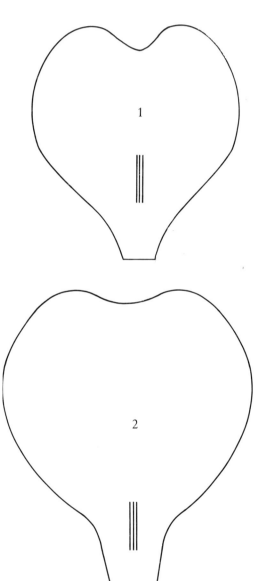

Step 1 To make the petals
Cut four petal shapes in metallic paper from pattern 1 and four larger petals in the same color from pattern 2.
Cup each petal, shiny side inwards, and curl the edges back over a knitting needle.

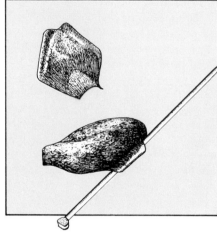

Step 2 To assemble flower
Dab glue on the top of the poppy seed head or roll of crêpe paper and dip it into the glitter.

First arrange the small petals evenly around the poppy seed head, with shiny sides on the inside, so that the curled edges curl outwards.
Put a dab of glue on the base of each petal to ensure that all hold firmly to center.
Bind the base of the petals to the stalk, just underneath the poppy seed head, with two twists of No. 3 wire.
Then arrange the four larger petals in the gaps around the flower and bind again with No. 3 wire to secure.
Open the petals out so that only the shiny center of the flower can be seen.
Bind the base of the flower with crêpe paper to cover join, if desired.

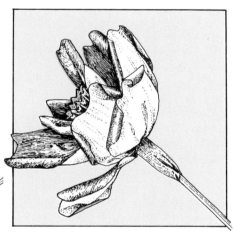

The natural color of the stalk can be left, but if you are using wire, cover with crêpe paper strip in the usual way.

—CHRISTMAS DECORATIONS—

For Christmas decorations and arrangements make Christmas roses and poinsettias in multi-colored foil as well as the more traditional red, pink and white crêpe paper. For the flower centers and stems use poppy seed heads on stalks, dipping the tops into glitter as for the metallic rose. Arrange the flowers with fir cones and leaves that have been sprayed silver or gold, and for a touch of extra color add a few bright baubles.

Real leaves make pretty foliage for your fantasy flowers. Gather prettily shaped leaves in the early summer when they are at their best (beech leaves and evergreens are very effective) and soak in one part glycerine to two parts hot water for two weeks. Take out and allow to dry. If misshapen, press flat under a heavy book. These leaves will remain fresh-looking and unbrittle for years.

For the Christmas table make several red or pink roses and arrange them in a flat dish in the center of the table. (The flowers will not need stems.) Make rose leaves in silver foil to go around the flowers. Sprinkle your arrangement with glitter and choose red or pink table napkins to match the flowers.

Arrange Christmas roses with holly that has been sprayed gold. Make shiny berries out of scrap paper rolled into balls and covered with squares (as for the anemone centre) of red tin foil or red crêpe paper sprayed with artist's varnish.

Another kind of berry to make is a shiny blackberry. First cut a 30–45cm (12–18in.) piece of No. 1 wire and make a hook at one end. Put a touch of glue on the hook and attach a ball of cotton wool (cotton) about the size of a marble. Dab glue all over the cotton wool ball.

In a saucer put some black hemp seeds (obtainable from a pet shop).

Roll the ball in the seeds so it is evenly covered and leave to dry. The berries can be left black or painted dark red, gold or silver. They must be varnished to make them shiny. Bind the stem with crêpe paper and varnish it too.

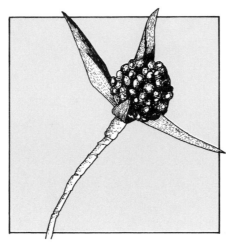

To make the **Christmas garland** fold and crumple 15–20cm (6–8in.) wide fine wire netting into a sausage shape. Fold this round into a circle not less than 45cm (18in.) in diameter as a foundation for your garland. Don't forget to make a hook of wire at the back so that you can hang it up! Fill your wire circle with natural greenery such as box, laurel, holly, ivy and berberis so that all the wire is covered. Now put poinsettias, Christmas roses and other Christmas glitter flowers into the wire on top of the greenery. Finish

the garland with a bright red satin or paper bow. Fabric or paper foliage is equally appropriate and looks best if sprayed with varnish to look shiny. The combination of real leaves and paper flowers, however, provides a more interesting mix of textures for this kind of arrangement.

The **tall cone of flowers**, fruit and preserved leaves standing by the window is specially arranged on a structure of fine wire netting and florist's foam. The wire netting can be shaped around a tall column of florist's foam to form a cone with a broad base. The arrangement in the picture was made to be viewed from the front and sides only. A smaller cone with a completely circular base could be made to stand on a table with flowers arranged all the way round it. The flower heads and fruits are attached to long lengths of strong No. 1 wire which is stuck through the wire netting into the florist's foam. The stems of the leaves are pushed through and supported by the wire.

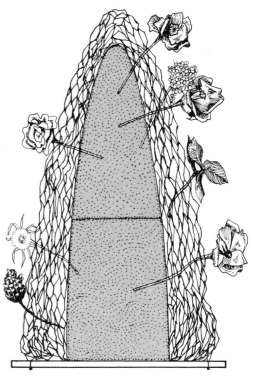

The splendid Christmas crackers are made even more so by having Christmas roses attached to them—which makes them almost too good to pull! The roses are attached to the center of the cracker with clear double-sided tape.

Christmas roses are beautifully delicate flowers to use as decorations for gift wrappings, particularly if they have been waxed. You may wish to wax a number of them to make an attractive arrangement for a table center.

EASTER

The Easter breakfast table is always exciting with its different kinds of bread and cake, and, of course, its colored and chocolate eggs in addition to all the everyday breakfast things. Flowers are a must on an occasion like this; with their fresh bright colors they create just the right air of festivity.

Primroses are pretty flowers—and versatile too! Individual flowers and leaves can be arranged around an Easter cake—simply place their stems under the cake or in the marzipan topping. Make them in fine yellow cotton fabric—ideal for springtime— with velvet leaves. Follow the instructions for polyanthus (they belong to the same flower family) made as a potted plant on page 132, although remember that here they are used singly.

Primroses can also decorate a napkin ring. Fix one to a ring by bending the flower stem under and around the edge of the ring, or by attaching the flower head without the stem to the ring with clear double-sided tape.

For the larger flowers, like narcissus, daffodil and crocus, scatter them singly or in pairs between place settings, or put them in a jug to give a glorious splash of color. The large chocolate Easter egg has a ribbon of primroses and waxed violets around it; these are fixed to the ribbon with clear double-sided tape.

Another idea for Easter for the slimmer who won't eat chocolate but still likes to receive an Easter gift, is a large decorated cardboard egg; trim it in the same way as the chocolate egg, but fill it with beautiful waxed flowers, which can then be arranged in a vase or worn—perhaps on an Easter bonnet!

PARTIES

Flowers that are cheerful and are quick and easy to make are ideal for children's or teenage parties. Mexican poppies and hollyhocks (see page 74) will provide a lot of fun for all the family too if they want to help you to make them. The big and beautiful paper poppies on the following pages were the first flowers that our author ever made—a move which has eventually resulted in this book.

Of all the flowers, Mexican poppies are the simplest and the most fun to make—and they're always popular.

Their charm may lie in the fact they are so different from real flowers. They are huge and bright, even garish, though of course this results from the gaily colored papers from which they are made. A very different effect could be achieved from a mixture of subtle pastel shades.

Some of the poppies in the picture are wired onto long pieces of cane which have been covered with crêpe paper and stuck into a firmly weighted flower pot. The result is a giant, growing Mexican poppy. Placed in rows these always look amusing—almost like sentries standing to attention. A pathway lined on either side with pots of poppies can make an inviting entrance to a party room, or placed either side of the doorway they provide a colorful and cheery welcome.

Another idea for a big single splash of color is to make a tall standing bush of flower heads. Large peonies, full blown roses and poppies can be stuck into a rounded shape of florist's foam to form a ball of flowers, approximately 45cm (18in.) in diameter. This is then put onto the top of a cane, either painted or covered in green crêpe paper, which has been planted firmly in a large flower pot. You will need sand or even soil to weight the pot so that the flowers are not top heavy.

Flowers made from shiny paper for Christmas mixed with fun fruits and leaves are also very suitable for this kind of arrangement. The more unreal they look and the brighter their colors, the better.

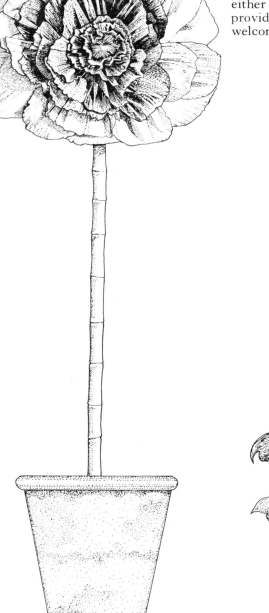

Mexican poppy

This is an enormous, brightly colored fun flower which is very quick and easy to make.

Choose any three colors of crêpe paper that you think go well together. Prepare the paper so that the colors run into each other and the paper becomes crinkly when dry.

You will need:
Prepared crêpe paper in chosen colors
No. 1 and No. 3 wire
Sisal twine
Scissors
Quick-drying clear glue
Wire cutters
Piece of hollow cane (optional)

Step 1 To make the petal strips
Cut three different colors of prepared crêpe paper in the following sizes:
First, 20cm (8in.) deep by 260cm (8½ft) long.
Second, 15cm (6in.) deep and the same length as above.
Third, 10cm (4in.) deep and half the above length.
Take the 20cm (8in.) strip and fold into lengths 11cm (4½in.) wide.
Cut through the several thicknesses of paper to round off the corners and make a V-shape in the center.
Unfold into a long strip of petals.
Repeat for the 15cm (6in.) strip.

Step 2 To make the stamens
Cut a piece of twine 10cm (4in.) long and separate out the strands at one end.

Step 3 To assemble the flower
Take the 10cm (4in.) strip and fold and pleat it around the stamens.

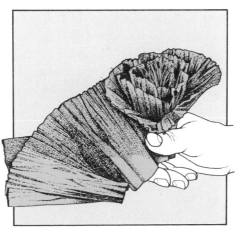

Bind two twists of No. 3 wire around the base to secure.
Repeat with the 15cm (6in.) strip, being careful to arrange the petals evenly.
Bind at base to secure.

Now repeat with the 20cm (8in.) strip and bind around base very tightly with No. 3 wire. If necessary, add a touch of glue to the base of the last petal so that it sticks to the petal strip.

Step 4 To make the stem
Cut a piece of No. 1 wire about 15cm (6in.) long and make a hook at one end.
Push unhooked end of wire down through the center of the flower so that the hook becomes embedded in the calyx.
Trim the thick base of the petals with a pair of scissors so that the paper tapers neatly into the stem.
Wrap a strip of green crêpe paper, 3.5cm (1½in.) wide, firmly around the flower base.

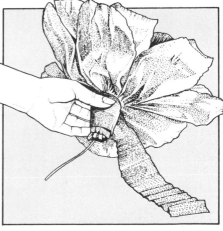

The stem wire can now be put inside a piece of cane if you want a tall upstanding flower.

Step 5 Finishing touches
Stretch each outer petal across its broadest part to make the tip turn inwards.
Bend flower head forward on its stem.

An essential requirement for any party, particularly for children, is that it should be colorful. These poppies certainly help to set the party scene.

WEDDINGS

Most of the flowers in the pictures on pages 158–9 are made from crêpe paper, except for the cotton fabric forget-me-nots and the cotton and organza rosebuds on the cake. The bride's bouquet is made from lace. Real foliage and everlasting flowers, heather and statice, are used to fill out the garlands.

The **garland for the table** is made from paper roses and rosebuds; tiny blue cornflowers and some smaller peonies have also been added. The stems for these flowers were made from No. 3 wire instead of the stronger No. 1 wire. These are covered with crêpe paper strip and then the stems are twisted together to form the garland, rather like a daisy chain. In order to hide the stems and fill in the spaces between the flowers, twist the short flower

stems of smaller flowers, such as rosebuds and cornflowers, into the garland.

Take care to allow the flower heads to stand free from the garland by leaving approximately 5cm (2in.) of stem which is not twisted into the other stems. This allows the flower heads to be arranged as desired once the garland is in position.

You should judge the length of your garland carefully according to the size of the table you are using and the size of the garland loops you think will look best. The one in the picture is made from several short lengths of garland, each forming a separate loop. Attach these at each end to the table cloth with pins, or by careful stitching to the cloth itself, or with a drawing pin that is strong enough to go through the cloth to the table underneath. Secure the table cloth with a drawing pin at each corner so that the weight of the garland does not pull it out of position.

The **garlands for the staircase** are made from paper peonies and

stephanotis, with pink and white heather and statice as well as real laurel leaves to fill out the spaces between the paper flowers and make a pretty feathery background to display them against.

The garland is built up around a structure of wire netting into which the stems of the flowers and leaves are carefully placed. The wire netting is attached to the staircase at intervals with No. 3 wire. You may find it easier to attach the wire in position first before you arrange the flowers in it.

The **wedding cake decoration** is made from a cone of florist's foam which has been carefully secured with No. 3 wire to a tall narrow-necked silver vase. The colored streamers are arranged all around the base of the foam by means of toothpicks: wind the end of each ribbon round half a toothpick and then push the toothpick with the ribbon into the foam. Finally stick the flowers all over the cone to form a decorative ball of flowers. Pink cornflowers and daisies decorate the different layers of the cake; only the flower heads are used. When the cake is to be cut, the cone of flowers, with or without its streamers, looks very pretty as a table decoration.

A **ball of flowers**, made in much the same way as this cake decoration, could also be used as a small bouquet for a bridesmaid. Simply cut the florist's foam to a rounded shape instead of a cone and have the streamers, or a bow, if preferred, falling from the base. Encircle the ball with No. 3 wire before putting the flowers into it and then tie a ribbon to the wire to form a loop for it to hang by, or use No. 1 wire to make a more rigid handle for carrying the bouquet. In this case take a 30cm (12in.) length of No. 1 wire and make a gentle curve 6cm (2½in.) from the end and cover the

wire with floral tape. Carefully insert the curved end of the wire into the central part of the ball of florist's foam so that the straight end of the wire protrudes to form a handle. The flowers can then be put into the foam to cover it completely.

When deciding on the color scheme for the flowers for a special occasion, such as a wedding, relate it to the other colors which have been chosen for the clothes and decorations. The joy of these handmade flowers is that you can confidently make and arrange them well before the day, if you wish. You can put the garlands in position when they are made and know that you will not have to worry about them dying. And you can use the flowers you like best, regardless of whether they are in season or not.

Lace bouquet

This wedding bouquet is a mixture of lace flowers and living foliage. The flowers can be made in silk or organza. The foliage too can be made in fabric.

You will need:
Lace strips 3.5cm (1½in.) wide
No. 3 wire
Green floral tape
Ivy leaves (or other leaves of choice)
Needle and thread
Stamens from a hobby shop

Step 1 To make the lace flowers
Cut lace into 30cm (12in.) strips. Cut 25cm (10in.) lengths of No. 3 wire. Fold wire in half with four or five stamens placed in the bend of the fold, and twist ends together.

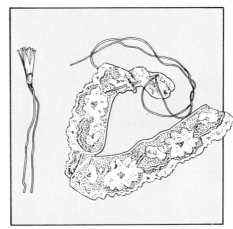

Gather one edge of a lace strip with needle and thread, place the stamens in the center of the lace, bunch up the lace around the stamens in the shape of a small flower and sew with a few stitches to secure in place.
Bind wire with green floral tape.
Repeat to make ten flowers.

Step 2 To assemble bouquet
Arrange flowers as desired by twisting their stems together. Entwine the ivy stems with the wire so that the ivy leaves form a triangular shape.
Bind stems all together at the back with floral tape and arrange flowers at the front to cover completely all the stems.

157

A wedding—what a chance for a celebration with flowers. Garlands of roses and rosebuds around the table, peonies and stephanotis on the staircase, azaleas and apple blossom in a large splendid arrangement, and cornflowers in an elegant swan-shaped vase. The cake is decorated with forget-me-nots, orange blossom, rosebuds, cornflowers and daisies. The bridal bouquet is made from creamy lace roses. These in themselves are good enough reason to open those bottles of champagne!

Index

Terms in constant use within the instructions are not entered each time in the index. The reader is referred to where they are explained in the introductory section. Entries in italic refer to illustrations.